MASTERING THE GEORGIA

3RD GRADE

CRCT

IN

SOCIAL STUDIES

Developed to the Georgia Performance Standards

Kindred Howard
Katie Herman

American Book Company
PO Box 2638
Woodstock, GA 30188-1383
Toll Free: 1 (888) 264-5877   Phone: (770) 928-2834
Fax: (770) 928-7483   Toll Free Fax: 1 (866) 827-3240
www.americanbookcompany.com

ACKNOWLEDGEMENTS

The authors would like to gratefully acknowledge the formatting and technical contributions of Becky Wright and Marsha Torrens.

We also want to thank Charisse Johnson and Eric Field for developing the graphics for this book.

This product/publication includes images from CorelDRAW 9 and 11 which are protected by the copyright laws of the United States, Canada, and elsewhere. Used under license.

PREFACE

Mastering the Georgia 3rd Grade CRCT in Social Studies will help students who are learning or reviewing material for the CRCT. The materials in this book are based on the testing standards as published by the Georgia Department of Education. This book is written to the grade 3 level, corresponding to approximately 500L to 700L on the Lexile text measure scale.

This book contains several sections. These sections are as follows: 1) general information about the book; 2) a diagnostic test; 3) an evaluation chart; 4) chapters that teach the concepts and skills that improve graduation readiness; 5) two practice tests. Answers to the tests and exercises are in a separate manual. The answer manual also contains a Chart of Standards for teachers to make a more precise diagnosis of student needs and assignments.

We welcome comments and suggestions about the book. Please contact the authors at

American Book Company
PO Box 2638
Woodstock, GA 30188-1383

Toll Free: 1 (888) 264-5877
Phone: (770) 928-2834
Fax: (770) 928-7483
Web site: www.americanbookcompany.com

ABOUT THE AUTHORS

Lead Author:

Kindred Howard is a 1991 alumnus of the University of North Carolina at Chapel Hill, where he graduated with a B.S. in Criminal Justice and national honors in Political Science. In addition to two years as a probation and parole officer in North Carolina, he has served for over twelve years as a teacher and writer in the fields of religion and social studies. His experience includes teaching students at both the college and high school level, as well as speaking at numerous seminars. He is the author of several books on U.S. history, American government, and economics. His books are currently used by public schools in Georgia, the Carolinas, Louisiana, and Maryland. In 2005, Mr. Howard received a national recognition of excellence for scoring in the top fifteen percent, all time, on the national Praxis II exam for social studies. He currently serves as the social studies coordinator for American Book Company and is completing a M.A. in history at Georgia State University. Mr. Howard lives in Kennesaw, Georgia, with his wife and three children.

Katie Herman is a graduate of Kennesaw State University, where she received a B.A. in English. She is the co-author of several books on history and social studies which are currently being used by public schools in Georgia and Louisiana. Ms. Herman currently works as a researcher and writer for American Book Company and plans to pursue a M.A. in professional writing. She lives in Woodstock, Georgia.

Georgia 3 Social Studies Diagnostic Test

The purpose of this diagnostic test is to measure your knowledge in social studies. This test is based on the GPS-based Georgia CRCT in Social Studies and adheres to the sample question format provided by the Georgia Department of Education.

General Directions:

1. Read all directions carefully.

2. Read each question or sample. Then, choose the best answer.

3. Choose only one answer for each question. If you change an answer, be sure to erase your original answer completely.

4. After taking the test, you or your instructor should score it using the evaluation chart following the test. Circle any questions you did not get correct and review those chapters.

1. The way that a building is designed is called   SS3H1

   A. Draco.   (C.) architecture.

   B. Parthenon.   D. democracy.

2. Jane was a white woman living in 1900. She wanted to have the   SS3H2
   same voting rights as men. Who would Jane have supported the
   most?

   A. Mary McLeod Bethune

   B. Eleanor Roosevelt

   C. Cesar Chavez

   (D.) Susan B. Anthony

✳ 3. Liberty, justice, and tolerance are all   SS3CG2

   A. guaranteed under the First Amendment.

   B. forms of expression.

   C. positive character traits.

   D. reserved powers.

✳ 4. Which of the following is **true**?   SS3E3

   A. Producers want to produce things that have a low price.

   B. Consumers want to buy things that have a high price.

   C. Producers have to spend money to produce things.

   D. Consumers will always pay high prices for goods.

5. Geography is the   SS3G1

   A. parallel line that runs around a globe.

   B. study of historical events.

   (C.) study of the earth and its people.

   D. northern half of the world.

6. The United States' national set of laws is called the   SS3CG1
   - A. Legislative.
   - B. General Assembly.
   - C. Bill of Rights.
   - D. Constitution.

7. The area that a building stands on is called   SS3E1
   - A. land.
   - B. a price.
   - C. a profit.
   - D. labor.

8. Which figure was **most** impacted by Boston, Massachusetts?   SS3G2
   - A. Frederick Douglass
   - B. Susan B. Anthony
   - C. Paul Revere
   - D. Cesar Chavez

9. The Olympic Games were invented by   SS3H1
   - A. United States citizens.
   - B. the ancient Greeks.
   - C. Cesar Chavez.
   - D. Thurgood Marshall.

10. What would be the **best** title for the list below?   SS3H2
   - Paul Revere
   - Frederick Douglass
   - Franklin Roosevelt

   - A. People Who Impacted the American Revolution
   - B. Leaders of the Abolitionist Movement
   - C. Famous U.S. Senators
   - D. People Who Have Impacted U.S. Democracy

11. The head of the <u>executive</u> branch of the <u>national</u> government is the   SS3CG1

   A. governor.

   B. president.

   C. Senate.

   D. House of Representatives.

12. Which of the following is provided by the government?   SS3E2

   A. bicycles   C. grocery stores

   B. fire departments   D. Wal-Mart

13. To be diligent means to   SS3CG2

   A. run for political office.

   B. be lazy.

   C. work hard and with great focus.

   D. tell the truth.

14. Ryan makes shirts for $25 each. He sells the shirts for $50. Ryan makes $25 per shirt. The $25 he makes is called   SS3E3

   A. tax.   C. price.

   B. fee.   D. profit.

15. A business that fixes peoples' cars is producing a   SS3E1

   A. fee.   C. service.

   B. good.   D. capital good.

16. Who was a strong political leader during World War II?   SS3H2

   A. Franklin Roosevelt

   B. Lyndon B. Johnson

   C. Cesar Chavez

   D. Paul Revere

17. Which branch of government is responsible for making sure that people follow the laws? SS3CG1

    A. legislative

    B. executive

    C. judicial

    D. Congress

Use the map below to answer questions 18, 19, and 20.

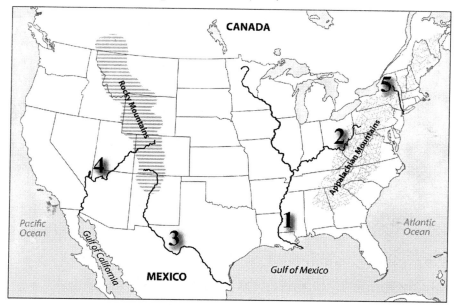

18. What does the number 2 represent on the map? SS3G1

    A. Hudson River

    B. Rio Grande River

    C. Ohio River

    D. Mississippi River

19. Which number represents the Rio Grande River? SS3G1

    A. 1

    B. 2

    C. 3

    D. 4

20. What does the number 1 represent on the map? SS3G1

    A. Hudson River

    B. Ohio River

    C. Mississippi River

    D. Colorado River

21. The Parthenon is an example of   SS3H1

   A. Greek Architecture.

   B. democracy.

   C. U.S. architecture.

   D. an Olympic event.

22. Why did the founders of the United States want a government   SS3CG1
    that included separation of powers?

   A. so the legislative branch would have the least amount of power

   B. so the judicial branch would have more power than the president

   C. so the executive branch would always have the most power

   D. so that no one leader or body of leaders would become too powerful

23. How did Thurgood Marshall show his belief in liberty?   SS3CG2

   A. He did not display liberty.

   B. by running for president of the United States

   C. by fighting for the rights of African Americans

   D. by warning American colonists that the British were coming

24. Goods that are used to produce other things are called   SS3E1

   A. entrepreneurs.

   B. labor.

   C. capital goods.

   D. taxes.

25. Rules set by the government are called   SS3H1

   A. democracies.   C. laws.

   B. civil rights.   D. columns.

26. What is the best title for the list below? SS3H2
    - The Great Society
    - Voting Rights Act of 1965
    - Wanted to end poverty

    A. Reasons for the United Nations

    B. Accomplishments of Franklin Roosevelt

    C. Goals of Lyndon B. Johnson

    D. Results of the New Deal

27. Jane loves the outdoors. She lives in Georgia. The closest SS3G1
    activity for her would be to

    A. sail on the Hudson River.

    B. hike in the Appalachian Mountains.

    C. snow ski in the Rockies.

    D. kayak on the Mississippi River.

28. The three levels of government are SS3CG1

    A. legislative, state, and town.

    B. executive, local, and county.

    C. national, local, and state.

    D. federal, state, and general.

29. Fees, fines, and taxes are SS3E2

    A. costs of being an entrepreneur.

    B. ways the government raises money.

    C. how consumers are paid.

    D. reasons people become entrepreneurs.

30. Eleanor Roosevelt fought for which of the following causes as first lady and a member of the U.N.?   SS3H2

    A. U.S. women's right to vote.

    B. the abolition of slavery.

    C. equal rights for minorities.

    D. to end the abolitionist movement.

Look at the map below and answer question 31.

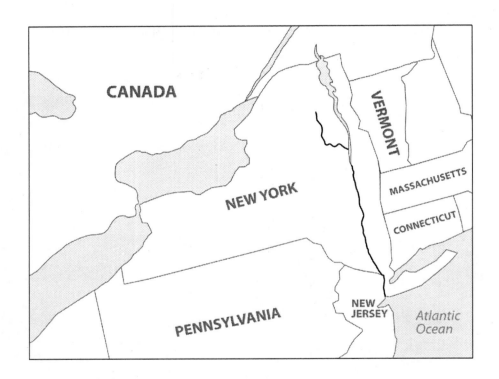

31. What geographic feature does the map show?   SS3G1

    A. Colorado River

    B. Grand Canyon

    C. Northwest Territory

    D. Hudson River

> It was built in Greece between 447 and 432 BC. It was a beautiful temple with classical columns.

32. What is the statement above describing?   SS3H1

    A. Monticello

    B. the White House

    C. the Parthenon

    D. the U.S. Capitol

33. On Election Day, U.S. citizens vote for people who will make   SS3H1
    government decisions. This is an example of

    A. direct democracy

    B. Greek architecture.

    C. Draco law.

    D. representative democracy.

34. If the majority of the Senate and the House of Representatives   SS3CG1
    passes a bill, it

    A. instantly becomes a law.

    B. must be signed by the president to become a law.

    C. is vetoed by Congress.

    D. is approved by the judicial branch.

35. In the U.S. economy, consumers and producers are   SS3E3

    A. interdependent.

    B. not important.

    C. not dependent on each other.

    D. not allowed to trade with each other.

36. Land, labor, capital, and entrepreneurship are   SS3E1

    A. important types of businesses.

    B. four types of resources.

    C. ways that the government raises money.

    D. things that people pay taxes on.

37. Paul Revere, Cesar Chavez, and Frederick Douglass were   SS3CG2

    A. leaders of the abolitionist movement.

    B. people who did not accept unjust authority.

    C. leaders of the United Nations.

    D. people who supported British rule.

38. John lives in Colorado. Of the following rivers, which is closest   SS3G1
to where John lives?

    A. Ohio   C. Hudson

    B. Rio Grande   D. Mississippi

39. Jennifer makes $200 a week. If Jennifer keeps her money to use   SS3E4
later, she will be

    A. spending her money.

    B. saving her money.

    C. changing her currency.

    D. making a profit.

40. The first African American to become a judge on the Supreme   SS3H2
Court was

    A. Thurgood Marshall.

    B. Lyndon B. Johnson.

    C. Frederick Douglass.

    D. Franklin Roosevelt.

41. People have to pay the government money to drive on a toll road. This is called a   SS3E2

    A. profit.   C. fee.

    B. fine.   D. service.

42. The Parthenon had a great impact on   SS3H1

    A. women's suffrage.

    B. representative democracy.

    C. Paul Revere's midnight ride.

    D. the U.S. Supreme Court Building.

Use this map to answer question 43.

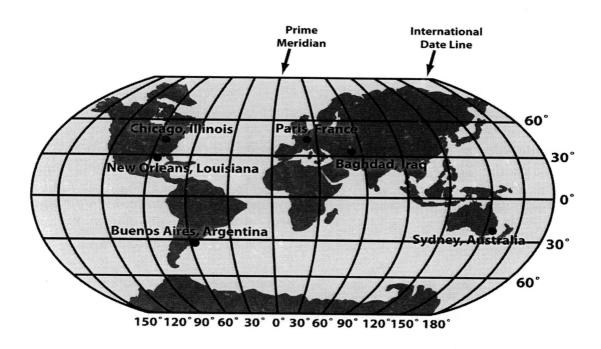

43. Which of the cities labeled on the map is closest to the equator?   SS3G1

    A. Chicago   C. Baghdad

    B. Paris   D. Sydney

44. Bikes, toys, computers, and clothes are all   SS3E1
    A. services.   C. consumers.
    B. producers.   D. goods.

45. How many United States senators does each state have?   SS3CG1
    A. one
    B. two
    C. three
    D. It depends on the population of the state.

46. Which of the following is an example of a direct democracy?   SS3H1
    A. Kelly does not get to vote in any elections.
    B. Tanya refuses to obey the law.
    C. Brian votes for Heather who will make decisions for him.
    D. Every qualified citizen gets to vote directly on each law and policy.

47. Paul Revere   SS3H2
    A. helped slaves escape.
    B. warned colonists that the British were coming during the Revolution.
    C. started a school for African Americans.
    D. created the New Deal to help the U.S. economy.

48. Which of the following is **true?**   SS3G1
    A. The Ohio River runs from New Mexico to Canada.
    B. The Ohio River is the longest river in the United States.
    C. The Ohio River is a tributary of the Colorado River.
    D. The Ohio River runs from Pennsylvania to Illinois.

49. When the president of France meets with a member of the U.S. government, it will **most likely** be with someone in the
    SS3CG1
    A. judicial branch.   C. executive branch.

    B. legislative branch.   D. Congress

50. Who serves as Georgia's chief executive?
    SS3CG1
    A. a mayor   C. the governor

    B. a senator   D. the president

51. Mary McLeod Bethune
    SS3H2
    A. was a migrant farm worker.

    B. was the first woman to vote.

    C. started a school for African American students.

    D. wrote the New Deal.

52. Jack is making an outline for a school report. What should go where the question mark below is?
    SS3H1
    A. Direct Democracy

        1.   ?

        2. Free adult males over the age of 18 could vote on issues

    A. Part of the Olympic Games

    B. Began in Athens, Greece

    C. The form of government found in the United States

    D. The reason ancient Greece built the Parthenon

53. Your parents probably go to work everyday. They provide
    SS3E1
    A. land.   C. the economy.

    B. profit.   D. labor.

54. Which of the following is **true**? SS3G1

    A. The Ohio River is located in New York.

    B. The Appalachian Mountains are located in the western United States.

    C. The Rocky Mountains run from New Mexico to Canada.

    D. The Colorado River separates eastern and western United States.

55. The imaginary line that runs around the earth at its center is called SS3G1

    A. the meridian.   C. the parallel line.

    B. the equator.   D. the hemisphere.

56. Which of the following is an example of paying a fine? SS3E2

    A. going out to dinner at an expensive restaurant

    B. giving a friend $25

    C. spending extra money on groceries this week

    D. paying the county $100 because you littered in the park

57. What do the Senate and the House of Representatives have in common? SS3CG1

    A. They have nothing in common.

    B. They are both part of Congress.

    C. They perform all the same duties.

    D. They are both part of the executive branch.

58. Who became an important leader in the abolitionist movement? SS3H2

    A. Cesar Chavez

    B. Paul Revere

    C. Frederick Douglass

    D. Lyndon B. Johnson

59. An entrepreneur is someone who   SS3E1

    A. works for the government.

    B. buys things.

    C. starts a business.

    D. works for a large company.

60. Which river divides the eastern and western United States?   SS3G1

    A. Hudson   C. Colorado

    B. Mississippi   D. Rio Grande

61. Lines of longitude are called   SS3G1

    A. international lines.

    B. parallels.

    C. meridians.

    D. equators.

62. The judicial branch of government is responsible for   SS3CG1

    A. making sure people follow the laws.

    B. making the laws.

    C. making sure laws are fair and constitutional.

    D. making the state laws.

63. Jennifer is excited because she will get to cast her vote on   SS3H2
Election Day. Who of the following is remembered for fighting
to give Jennifer this right?

    A. Franklin Roosevelt

    B. Eleanor Roosevelt

    C. Mary McLeod Bethune

    D. Susan B. Anthony

64. Julie needs to choose a title for the following list. Which title would be the best? SS3CG1

- House of Representatives
- Senate
- Makes the laws

A. Executive Branch of Government

B. Judicial Branch of Government

C. Legislative Branch of Government

D. General Assembly

65. Which of these people would have been most grateful for Cesar Chavez during the 1960s? SS3H2

A. an African American slave

B. a poor farm worker

C. a woman that wanted to vote

D. a southern business owner

66. Parallels are SS3G1

A. lines of latitude.

B. only found in the Eastern Hemisphere.

C. lines that run north and south.

D. lines of longitude.

67. The U.S. Congress is divided into two houses. Which house consists of two representatives from each state, no matter what the population of the state? SS3CG1

A. the House of Representatives

B. the Senate

C. the president's cabinet

D. the judicial branch

Read the statement below and answer the following question.

> This United States leader is the head of the executive branch. He or she enforces laws, deals with other countries, sets policies, and is the leader of the nation's military.

68. Who is the statement above describing?   SS3CG1

    A. the chief justice of the Supreme Court

    B. the vice president of the United States

    C. the president of the United States

    D. the governor of the United States

69. Which of the following is **true**?   SS3H2

    A. Paul Revere lived in fear of being returned as a slave to the South.

    B. Paul Revere could have been arrested and hanged by the British.

    C. Paul Revere was often threatened by members of the Ku Klux Klan.

    D. Paul Revere was often ignored as he spoke about women's rights.

70. What is the **best** title for the list below?   SS3CG1
    - Secretary of State
    - Secretary of Defense
    - Secretary of the Treasury

    A. Chief Justices on the Supreme Court

    B. Leaders of the General Assembly

    C. Members of the President's Cabinet

    D. Positions of the Judicial Branch

EVALUATION CHART FOR GEORGIA GRADE 3 CRCT IN SOCIAL STUDIES

Directions: On the following chart, circle the question numbers that you answered incorrectly and evaluate the results. These questions are based on the Georgia Competency Standards. Then turn to the appropriate topics (listed by chapters), read the explanations, and complete the exercises. Review other chapters as needed. Finally, complete the practice test(s) to assess your progress and further prepare you for the **Georgia Grade 3 Social Studies Test**.

Note: Some question numbers will appear under multiple chapters because those questions require demonstration of multiple skills.

Chapter	Diagnostic Test Question
1. Historical Understandings of U.S. Democracy	1, 2, 9, 10, 16, 21, 25, 26, 30, 32, 33, 40, 42, 46, 47, 51, 52, 58, 63, 65, 69
2. Geographic Understandings	5, 8, 18, 19, 20, 27, 31, 38, 43, 48, 54, 55, 57, 60, 61, 66
3. United States Government and Civics	3, 6, 11, 13, 17, 22, 23, 28, 34, 45, 49, 50, 62, 64, 67, 68, 70
4. Economic Understandings	4, 7, 12, 14, 15, 24, 29, 35, 36, 39, 41, 44, 53, 56, 59

Chapter 1
Historical Understandings
of U.S. Democracy

This chapter addresses the following GPS-based CRCT standard(s):

SS3H1	The student will explain the political roots of our modern democracy in the United States of America.
SS3H2	The student will discuss the lives of Americans who expanded people's rights and freedoms in a democracy.

1.1 THE IMPACT OF ANCIENT GREECE ON THE UNITED STATES

ARCHITECTURE

The way buildings are built and designed is called **architecture**. The ancient Greeks became famous for a form of architecture called classical. Classical architecture is known for its columns. **Columns** are large poles that support buildings. Classical columns stood at the front entrances of buildings, making the buildings look magnificent. Classical architecture made the Greeks seem powerful and impressive. The most famous example of Greek architecture is the **Parthenon.** The ancient Greeks built it as a temple between 447 and 432 BC.

Parthenon

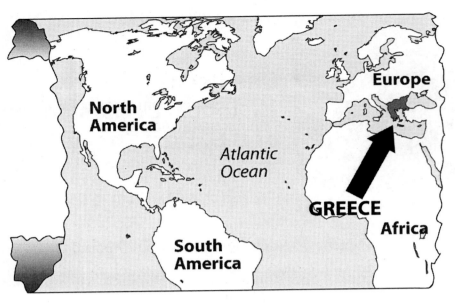

Map of Greece

American builders also used classic architecture when building many government buildings. U.S. leaders wanted buildings that showed power and confidence. Below are photos of several U.S. buildings that imitate the Greeks' classic style. Notice their use of columns. Compare them to the previous picture of the Parthenon.

Thomas Jefferson's Virginia Home, Monticello

The U.S. Supreme Court Building

The White House

The U.S. Capitol

THE OLYMPICS

The ancient Greeks held the first **Olympic Games**. The Olympics is a series of sporting events. The games began in 776 BC in Olympia, Greece. Greeks from different city-states (cities with their own king and surrounding villages) competed against each other. These games were held until AD 393. The modern Olympic Games began in 1896. Athletes from all over the world gather every four years to compete in both summer and winter games.

Ancient Olympics

Modern Olympics

DEMOCRACY

One of the world's first democracies began in Athens, Greece, around 500 BC. A **democracy** is a government ruled by the people. Citizens vote to make decisions. Athens was a direct democracy. In a **direct democracy**, any qualified citizen may vote directly on law and policy. Free adult males over the age of eighteen could vote in Athens. The ancient Greeks called this type of

Ancient Greek Democracy

government Athenian democracy. They believed that each community should choose its own leaders and set its own rules.

Today, the United States is also a democracy. But it is a representative democracy. In a **representative democracy**, people elect representatives to vote on issues and policies for them. The United States used the ancient ideas of the Greeks to create its own democratic government.

LAW

For a long time, the Greeks had no written laws. **Laws** are rules set by the government. If people do not obey laws, then the government punishes them. In 629 BC, a leader named Draco wrote Greece's first **constitution** (set of laws). His laws could be read by all citizens. People could finally know what the law said and how to punish those who broke the law. Some of his punishments were

Constitutional Convention

very harsh. But Draco's laws made it easier to apply the law fairly.

Over two thousand years later, the United States adopted a written set of laws called the **United States Constitution**. The Constitution limits the powers of the government by stating what it can, and cannot, do. It also protects people's rights. Like Draco's laws, the U.S. Constitution gives people a written code to live by. U.S. states also have state constitutions. State constitutions are also based on Draco's idea that it is important to have written laws.

Practice 1.1: The Impact of Ancient Greece on the United States

1. The Parthenon is an example of

    A. democracy.   C. Greek architecture.

    B. U.S. architecture.   D. Draco's laws.

2. The United States and ancient Greece are different in that

    A. the United States is a direct democracy, but Greece was a representative democracy.

    B. the United States is a representative democracy, but Greece was a direct democracy.

    C. the United States has a Constitution, but Greece never had written laws.

    D. Greek athletes compete in the Olympics every four years, but U.S. athletes don't.

3. Which of the following is an example of representative democracy?

   A. As a citizen, Bill gets to vote on every issue that comes before Congress.

   B. Anna does not get to vote in any elections.

   C. Brian writes a set of laws.

   D. Antonio votes for Susan, who will make decisions for him in Congress.

1.2 PEOPLE WHO HAVE IMPACTED U.S. DEMOCRACY

People who have lived in the past are known as historical figures. Many historical figures have tried to protect democratic rights and freedoms.

PAUL REVERE

Boston Massacre

Paul Revere's Midnight Ride

Paul Revere lived at the time of the American Revolution. He wanted the colonies to be independent (free) of Great Britain. Like many, Revere wanted the colonists to form their own country. He made a famous engraving (picture) of the Boston Massacre that led many other colonists to want independence too. (The Boston Massacre was the name given to an important event in Boston, Massachusetts. During the "massacre," British soldiers shot several colonists.) When the Revolution finally started, Revere and other messengers rode their horses through the night to warn colonists that the British were coming. Revere is most remembered for this midnight ride. His warning helped John Hancock and Samuel Adams escape capture. Both of these men were important leaders in America's fight for independence.

FREDERICK DOUGLAS

Frederick Douglass was an African American who lived during the 1800s. He was an important civil rights activist. (**Civil rights** are rights that all citizens have. In the United States, citizens' civil rights are protected by the Constitution.) Douglass grew up as a slave in the South. As an adult, he escaped to the North and became free. Douglass educated himself and became an important leader in the **abolitionist movement**. The abolitionist movement wanted to end slavery. Douglass was a powerful speaker who fought for the civil rights of slaves. He is often called the founder of the American civil rights movement.

Frederick Douglass

SUSAN B. ANTHONY

Women's Suffrage March

S.B. Anthony

For many years, women in the United States were not granted the same rights as men. One right that women did not have was the right to vote. **Susan B. Anthony** was a strong supporter of women's rights. She is best known as a leader of the **women's suffrage movement**. (Suffrage means the right to vote.) Even after she died in 1906, many of her followers kept fighting for suffrage. In 1920, U.S. women finally won the right to vote.

MARY MCLEOD BETHUNE

Mary McLeod Bethune was an educator and civil rights leader. She is best known for starting a school for African American students. The school was successful and became known as Bethune-Cookman College. In 1936, President Franklin Roosevelt made Bethune one of his advisors.

M.M. Bethune

FRANKLIN ROOSEVELT

In 1932, **Franklin Roosevelt** became president of the United States. He entered office during a very hard time. The nation's economy was hurting. Many U.S. citizens were out of work. Even many people who were once rich lost their homes and became poor. This period was known as the Great Depression. Roosevelt came up with a plan to fix the country's problems. It was called the **New Deal**. Under the New Deal, the government spent money to make jobs and help the poor. It helped people make it through some of the nation's toughest times.

Children during the Great Depression

FDR & Eleanor Roosevelt

President Roosevelt also led the country through **World War II**. The war got its name because it was the second war in twenty-five years to involve many countries. Roosevelt was a strong leader during the war. Under his leadership, the United States and its allies (friends) defeated Germany and Japan. Victory in the war helped protect democracy and freedom in the United States and other countries.

ELEANOR ROOSEVELT

Eleanor Roosevelt was the wife of President Franklin Roosevelt. She supported human rights. **Human rights** are rights that belong to every person and should not be taken away by the government. Eleanor Roosevelt wanted equal rights for minorities (nonwhites) and women. She even got her husband to include help for women in some of his New Deal programs.

After President Roosevelt died, the new president named Eleanor as the US delegate (representative) to the United Nations. The **United Nations** (UN) was formed after World War II. Many countries are members. These countries try to prevent wars and meet the needs of people around the world. While a member of the UN, Roosevelt helped write a special declaration on human rights. It was the first document signed by many countries to state that all people have human rights.

THURGOOD MARSHALL

Before the 1960s, many places in the United States were segregated. Segregation means that the law required blacks and whites to remain separate. They could not eat in the same areas at restaurants. They could not use the same waiting rooms or public restrooms. They were not allowed to sit next to each other on buses. White and black children could not even go to the same schools. Since whites were in power, African Americans suffered under segregation. One area where they suffered was in education. Black schools were not as good as white

Thurgood Marshall

schools. **Thurgood Marshall** was a lawyer who fought for civil rights. In a court case called *Brown v. Board of Education*, Marshall got the Supreme Court (the country's highest court) to say that segregation in public schools is illegal (against the law). Soon, segregation was not allowed in other places either. Marshall later became the first African American to sit as a judge on the Supreme Court.

LYNDON B. JOHNSON

Lyndon B. Johnson was president of the United States from 1963–1969. While he was president, Johnson wanted to end poverty in the United States. (When someone lives in poverty, it means that they are very poor.) He also wanted African Americans and other minorities to be treated fairly. He started a series of programs called the Great Society. These programs tried to help poor people. They provided money, education, and medical help. President Johnson also signed laws that protected civil rights. One of the most important laws he signed was the Voting Rights Act of 1965. This law made it easier for African Americans to vote. President Johnson helped open the door for more blacks to vote and serve in elected office.

Lyndon B. Johnson

CESAR CHAVEZ

Cesar Chavez was a Mexican American farm worker. He fought for rights for migrant workers. (Migrant workers are poor farm workers who move from place to place to find work harvesting crops. Many migrant workers are Hispanic.) Chavez founded the National Farm Workers Association and the United Farm Workers. For many years, Chavez protested poor working conditions and the use of dangerous pesticides. (Pesticides are used to kill bugs and protect crops. Sometimes, they can make farm workers sick.) Chavez helped win better pay and working conditiions for migrant workers.

Cesar Chavez

Migrant Worker

SOCIAL BARRIERS AND OBSTACLES

These historic figures faced many challenges. Paul Revere could have been arrested and hanged for taking part in the revolution. Frederick Douglass lived in fear of being captured and returned to slaveowners in the South. Mary McLeod Bethune was often threatened by members of the Ku Klux Klan. (The Ku Klux Klan supported violence and hatred of African Americans.) In the beginning, Susan B. Anthony was often ignored as she spoke about women's rights. People who stand up for democracy and freedom show great bravery and courage.

Practice 1.2: People Who Have Impacted U.S. Democracy

1. Paul Revere protected democracy and freedom by

    A. fighting for the civil rights of African Americans.

    B. helping migrant workers.

    C. supporting the American Revolution.

    D. taking part in the New Deal.

2. Match the historical figures listed below with the number of the cause they took part in

    _____ Eleanor Roosevelt   1. workers' rights

    _____ Cesar Chavez   2. women's suffrage

    _____ Lyndon Johnson   3. voting rights

    _____ Franklin Roosevelt   4. human rights

    _____ Susan B. Anthony   5. defeating foreign enemies

3. List some examples of obstacles and challenges that face some of the historic figures we learned about in section 1.2.

CHAPTER 1 REVIEW

Key Terms and People

architecture

columns

Parthenon

Olympic Games

democracy

direct democracy

representative democracy

laws

constitution

United States Constitution

Paul Revere

Frederick Douglass

civil rights

abolitionist movement

Susan B. Anthony

women's suffrage movement

Mary McLeod Bethune

Franklin Roosevelt

New Deal

World War II

Eleanor Roosevelt

human rights

United Nations

Thurgood Marshall

Lyndon B. Johnson

Cesar Chavez

Multiple Choice Questions

1. The United States Supreme Court building is an example of

   A. democracy in action.

   B. Greek architecture's impact on the United States.

   C. Draco's laws.

   D. representative democracy.

2. Read the quote below and answer the following question.

   > "The British are coming! The British are coming!"

   Who said these words?

   A. Frederick Douglass

   B. Susan B. Anthony

   C. Franklin Roosevelt

   D. Paul Revere

3. On Election Day, your mom and dad vote for people who will make government decisions. This is an example of
   A. direct democracy.
   B. draco law.
   C. representative democracy.
   D. Greek architecture.

4. The United States government is based on a written constitution. Who helped come up with the idea of written laws?
   A. Draco of Greece
   B. Lyndon B. Johnson
   C. Mary McLeod Bethune
   D. Paul Revere

5. George is a member of a group that thinks all people have rights, no matter what country they live. George's group is probably **most** grateful for
   A. the Parthenon.
   B. Frederick Douglass.
   C. Eleanor Roosevelt.
   D. Lyndon Johnson.

6. Megan is excited because she will get to cast her vote for president on Election Day. Who fought to help give Megan this right?
   A. Franklin Roosevelt
   B. Eleanor Roosevelt
   C. Mary McLeod Bethune
   D. Susan B. Anthony

7. Which of these people would have been **most** grateful for Cesar Chavez during the 1960s?
   A. Mexican American business owner
   B. African Americans fighting segregation
   C. poor farm worker
   D. woman hoping to vote

8. You probably have people of different races in your class at school. Who helped make sure that children of different races could go to the same schools?
   A. Lyndon B. Johnson
   B. Thurgood Marshall
   C. Frederick Douglass
   D. Susan B. Anthony

Chapter 2
Geographic Understandings

This chapter addresses the following GPS-based CRCT standard(s):

SS3G1	The student will locate major topographical features.
SS3G2	The student will describe the cultural and geographic systems associated with the historical figures in Ss3H2a.

2.1 MAJOR GEOGRAPHIC FEATURES IN THE UNITED STATES

Geography is the study of the earth and its peoples. Students are learning about geography when they study where places are located or how people live. Geography also includes the mountains, rivers, oceans, and other features that make up the earth's surface. In this chapter, we will study U.S. geography.

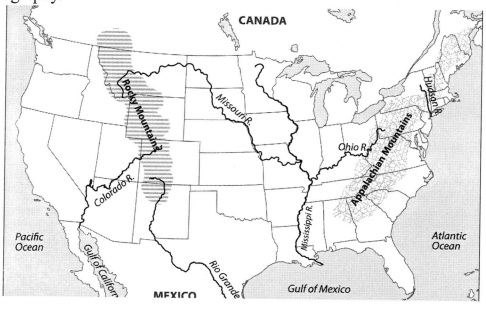

MAJOR RIVERS AND MOUNTAINS

Look at the map on the previous page. It shows where some of the United States' most important rivers and mountain ranges are located.

U.S. RIVERS

The **Mississippi River** runs from the state of Minnesota to the Gulf of Mexico. It is the second-longest river in the United States. The Mississippi River is one of the most important rivers in U.S. history. It allows travelers and goods to travel back and forth between the Gulf of Mexico to the central United States. Many major cities are located along the Mississippi. The river serves as a dividing line between the eastern and western United States.

Mississippi River

The **Ohio River** runs from Pennsylvania to Illinois. It is a tributary of the Mississippi River. (A tributary is a river that feeds water into another river.) For many years, the Ohio served as a boundary between the British colonies and Native American territory. After the American Revolution, white settlers moved into territory across the Ohio. This area was called the Northwest Territory. The government did not allow slavery in the Northwest Territory. For many years, the Ohio River served as a boundary between slave states (states that allowed slavery) and free states (states where slavery was illegal). It also played an important role in trade and commerce. People used the Ohio to travel and ship goods from eastern cities to western territories.

Lewis and Clark

The **Missouri River** is also a tributary of the Mississippi. It is the longest river in the United States. It runs from Montana to Missouri. The Missouri played an important role as people moved west. It allowed explorers to travel west by water. Later, it allowed travelers and traders to use boats to move from east to west.

The **Rio Grande** separates Texas from Mexico. It begins in Colorado and runs to the Gulf of Mexico.

The **Colorado River** runs from the state of Colorado to the Gulf of California in Mexico. Over millions of years, the river's flow has created the Grand Canyon. The Grand Canyon is a deep gorge located in Arizona.

The **Hudson River** runs through eastern New York. It meets the Atlantic Ocean at New York City. Native Americans and early Europeans used the river for travel and trade. Many early European explorers sailed up the Hudson because they thought it would take them all the way to the Pacific Ocean.

Colonial Hudson River Scene

U.S. MOUNTAIN RANGES

Daniel Boone

The **Appalachian Mountains** run from Georgia to southern Canada. Early British colonists had difficulty crossing the Appalachians. Over time, explorers like Daniel Boone helped pave the way across the mountain range. After the American Revolution, even more white settlers crossed the Appalachians. Many Native Americans lived in and beyond the Appalachian Mountains long before white American settlers arrived.

The **Rocky Mountains** are located in the western United States. They run from the state of New Mexico to western Canada. The Rockies were home to Native Americans for thousands of years before white Europeans arrived. Many white settlers moved to the region after people discovered gold during the seventeen and eighteen hundreds.

Rocky Mountains

Practice 2.1: Major Geographic Features in the United States

Look at the map below and answer the following question.

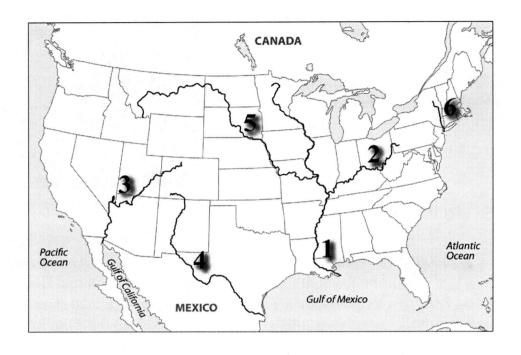

1. Write the correct number next to each of the rivers listed below.

    Mississippi _____   Hudson _____

    Missouri _____   Colorado _____

    Rio Grande _____   Ohio _____

2. The Appalachian Mountains are located in the
    A. eastern United States.

    B. western United States.

    C. Grand Canyon.

    D. Northwest Territory.

2.2 FINDING LOCATIONS ON MAPS AND GLOBES

UNDERSTANDING LATITUDE AND LONGITUDE

Globes are models of the earth. **Maps** are flat pictures of the earth, or some part of the earth. People use both to learn where places are located in the world. To help people locate places more easily, maps and globes have lines of **latitude** and lines of **longitude**. These are imaginary lines that make it easier to understand where places are. Lines of latitude run east-west and are called **parallels**. Look at the images below. The image on the left shows lines of latitude on a globe. The image on the right shows lines of latitude on a map.

Latitude on Globe

Latitude on Map

Lines of longitude run north-south from pole to pole. Lines of longitude are called **meridians**. The North Pole is located at the top of a world map or globe. The South Pole is located at the bottom of a world map or globe. Look at the images below. The image on the left shows lines of longitude on a globe. The image on the right shows lines of longitude on a map.

Longitude on Globe

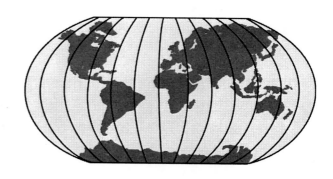

Longitude on Map

Image 1

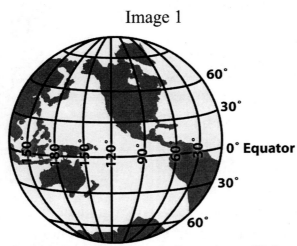

Latitude and Longitude Degrees on Globe

Latitude and longitude are measured by degrees. Look at images 1 and 2. Image 1 shows a globe with lines of latitude and longitude labeled by degrees. Image 2 shows a map with lines of latitude and longitude measured by degrees.

Image 2

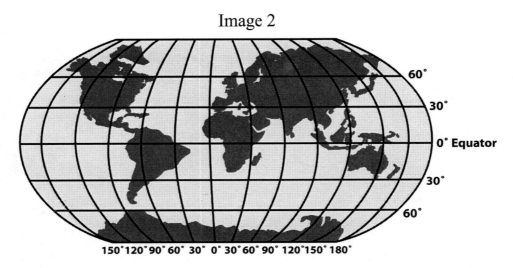

Latitude and Longitude Degrees on Map

The **equator** is the parallel (line of latitude) that runs around a globe or across a world map at its center. The equator is located at 0° latitude. Every parallel above the equator is in the **Northern Hemisphere** (northern half of the world). Every parallel below the equator is in the **Southern Hemisphere** (southern half of the world).

The **prime meridian** is a meridian (line of longitude) that runs from pole to pole through parts of Europe and Africa. It is located at 0° longitude. The **International Date Line** is the meridian located at 180° longitude. It is located directly opposite of the prime meridian on a globe. Every meridian west of the prime meridian up to the International Date Line is located in the **Western Hemisphere** (western half of the world). Every meridian located east of the prime meridian up to the International Date Line is located in the **Eastern Hemisphere**. Once people know the latitude and longitude of a place, they can find it easily on a map or globe.

USING LATITUDE AND LONGITUDE

In chapter 1, we learned about the influence Greece has had on U.S. democracy. Let's practice using lines of latitude and longitude by locating Athens, Greece, on a map (or globe). Look at the map below. Find the equator, prime meridian, and Athens, Greece. Athens is located roughly 38° north of the equator. It is also roughly 43° east of the prime meridian. Therefore, Athens is located at approximately 38° N, 43° E. Together, Athens' latitude and longitude tells us exactly where it is located in the world. Latitude and longitude can be used to locate any place in the world.

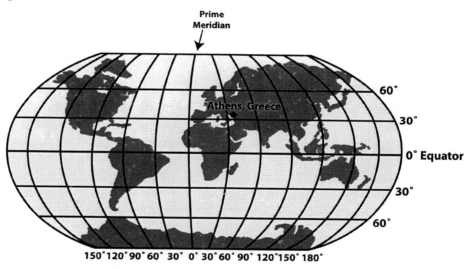

SYMBOLS for LATITUDE and LONGITUDE		
° = degrees	N = Northern Hemisphere	W = Western Hemisphere
	S = Southern Hemisphere	E = Eastern Hemisphere
EXAMPLES OF HOW TO WRITE LOCATIONS BASED ON LATITUDE AND LONGITUDE		
Location		Location Written Symbolically
Thirty-three degrees north latitude, Twenty-seven degrees west longitude:		33° N, 27°W
Fifty degrees south latitude, Thirty-five degrees east longitude:		50°S, 35°E

Practice 2.2:   Finding Location on Maps and Globes

Look at the images below to answer questions 1 through 4.

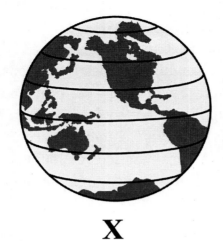   

X   **Y**

1.   Which image shows parallels?
   A. X   C. both

   B. Y   D. neither

2. Which image shows meridians?
   A. X   C. both

   B. Y   D. neither

3. On which image would one find the equator labeled?
   A. X   C. both

   B. Y   D. neither

4. Which image divides the world into hemispheres?
   A. X   C. both

   B. Y   D. neither

Look at the map below and answer question 5.

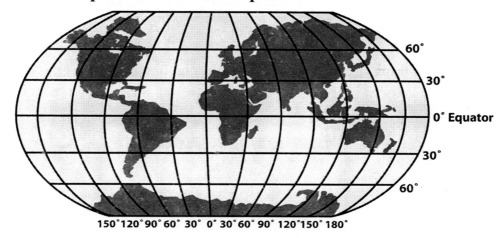

5. Which of the following is **closest** to where you live?

   A. 33° S, 80° W   C. 35° N, 80° E

   B. 33° N, 85° E   D. 30° N, 83° W

2.3 GEOGRAPHY AND U.S. HISTORY

Geography impacts U.S. History. The places people live help shape them and determine how they act. For example, Paul Revere lived in colonial Massachusetts. People in colonial Massachusetts favored independence, especially around Boston. It is not surprising that Revere helped the revolutionary cause through his engraving of the Boston Massacre and his midnight ride. The fact that the British marched from Boston to the Massachusetts countryside also helped Revere become famous. The geographic distance made it necessary for someone to warn the colonists by horseback. Geography helped Revere become a Patriot. It also helped provide a role that made him an important figure in U.S. history.

Practice 2.3:   Geography and U.S. History

Meet with a group of three or four classmates. Review the historical figures discussed in chapter 1, section 1.2. For each historical figure, write down three or four ways you think geography affected the role they played in U.S. history? Ask your teacher for help if necessary.

Paul Revere

CHAPTER 2 REVIEW

Key Terms and People

geography	globes	Southern Hemisphere
Mississippi River	maps	prime meridian
Ohio River	latitude	International Date Line
Missouri River	longitude	Western Hemisphere
Rio Grande	parallels	Eastern Hemisphere
Colorado River	meridians	
Hudson River	equator	
Appalachian Mountains	Northern Hemisphere	
Rocky Mountains		

Multiple Choice Questions

1. Which of the following is **true**?

   A. The Rocky Mountains serve as a dividing line between the eastern and western United States.

   B. The Mississippi River is an important river that runs north to south through the United States.

   C. The Ohio River separates the Northern Hemisphere from the Southern Hemisphere.

   D. The Colorado River separates Colorado from Mexico.

2. President Lyndon Johnson grew up poor in Texas. When Johnson became president, he began a "war on poverty." This is an example of

   A. latitude impacting longitude.

   B. environment affecting a historical figure.

   C. President Johnson being influenced by the Mississippi River.

   D. President Johnson's distrust of poor people.

3. If an explorer wanted to travel west by water along the southern edge of the Northwest Territory, then he or she should follow the
   A. Mississippi River.   C. Ohio River.

   B. Colorado River.   D. Rio Grande.

Look at the map below and answer question 4.

4. What geographic feature does the map show?
   A. Missouri River   C. Hudson River

   B. Mississippi River   D. Colorado River

Look at the map below and answer questions 5 and 6.

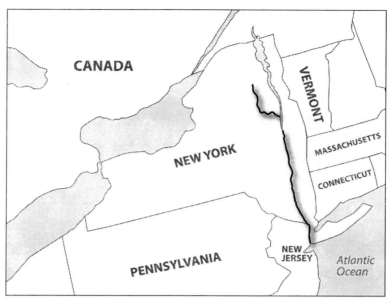

5. What geographic feature does the map show?

    A. Grand Canyon

    B. Hudson River

    C. Colorado River

    D. Rio Grande

6. Which of the following is a geographic feature that could also be shown on the map above?

    A. Rocky Mountains

    B. Paul Revere's ride

    C. Northwest Territory

    D. Appalachian Mountains

Look at the map below and answer questions 7 – 9.

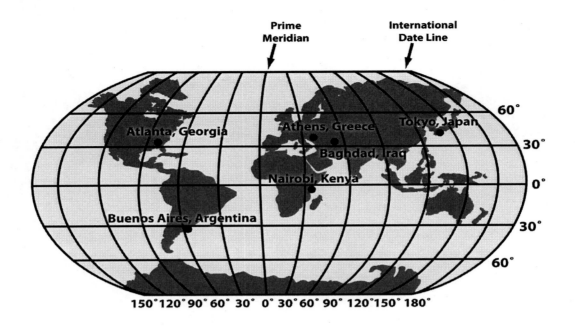

7. How many cities labeled on the map above are in the Southern Hemisphere?

    A. 1   B. 2   C. 3   D. 4

8. Which city on the map is **closest** to 40° N, 138° E?

    A. Athens   C. Baghdad

    B. Atlanta   D. Tokyo

9. Which city is located **closest** to the equator?

    A. Baghdad   C. Nairobi

    B. Atlanta   D. Tokyo

Chapter 3
United States Government and Civics

This chapter addresses the following GPS-based CRCT standard(s):

SS3CG1	The students will explain the importance of the basic principles that provide the foundation of a republican form of government.
SS3CG2	The student will discuss the character of different historical figures in SS3H2a.

3.1 PRINCIPLES OF REPUBLICAN GOVERNMENT

SEPARATION OF POWERS

In 1787, the United States' Founding Fathers wrote the **U.S. Constitution**. The Constitution is the nation's laws. The Constitution tells its readers how the U.S. government works. It sets up a government based on a **separation of powers**. Power does not rest with one ruler or group of rulers. Instead, the Constitution separates power by dividing it between three branches of government.

THREE BRANCHES OF THE NATIONAL GOVERNMENT

LEGISLATIVE BRANCH (CONGRESS)

The first branch of government is the **legislative branch**. The legislative branch makes laws. The national legislative branch is called **Congress**. It is made up of two houses. The **House of Representatives** is based

U.S. Capital

on population (how many people live in a state). States with more people have more representatives. Members of the House of Representatives serve two-year terms. The other house in Congress is the United States **Senate**. Each state has two senators. Members of the Senate serve six-year terms.

The legislative branch has other powers too. The Senate must okay treaties (agreements) with other countries. It must also okay public officials appointed by the president. The House has the power to impeach (charge with doing something wrong) the president and other public officials. These are just some of the powers held by the legislative branch.

EXECUTIVE BRANCH (PRESIDENT, VICE PRESIDENT, AND THE CABINET)

The **executive branch** enforces the nation's laws. Enforcement means making sure that federal laws are followed. The **president** of the United States heads the executive branch. He or she is the leader of the country. The president enforces laws, deals with other countries, sets policies, and is commander in chief (leader) of the nation's

White House

military. He or she can also **veto** laws passed by Congress. If the president vetoes a law, it does not become a law unless two-thirds of both houses of Congress vote in favor of it again. The president also appoints (names) federal judges and members of the cabinet.

President Lincoln

President Roosevelt

President Reagan

President Obama

Vice President Joe Biden

The **vice president** is the second-highest executive. He or she leads the Senate. But he or she only votes in the Senate if there is a tie to break. If the president dies or is unable to finish his or her term, then the vice president becomes president. Both the president and the vice president serve four-year terms.

The executive branch also includes the president's **cabinet**. The cabinet is not mentioned in the Constitution. It formed over time to help the president carry out executive duties. Cabinet members give the president advice and are in charge of different parts of the executive branch. Below is a table listing some cabinet members.

CABINET POSITION	EXECUTIVE RESPONSIBILITIES
Secretary of State	U.S. relations with other countries
Secretary of Defense	U.S. military
Attorney General	U.S. law enforcement
Secretary of the Treasury	U.S. economy and government money

JUDICIAL BRANCH (FEDERAL COURTS)

Supreme Court Building

The **judicial branch** is made up of courts. The courts make sure that laws follow the Constitution and are applied fairly. The highest court in the country is the **United States Supreme Court**. The president appoints members of the Supreme Court and all lower federal courts. Nine justices (judges) sit on the Supreme Court. The lead justice is called the **chief justice**. The other eight justices are called associate justices. The Supreme Court mostly hears **appeals**. An appeal is a court case that has already been decided by a lower court. It is reviewed by the Supreme Court to make sure that the case was decided correctly and that all laws were followed.

US Supreme Court Members, 2008

LEVELS OF GOVERNMENT

STATE GOVERNMENT

In the United States, there are different levels of government. The **federal government** is the national government (Congress, the president, and the federal courts). **State governments** are responsible for state laws. In Georgia, the legislative branch is called the **General Assembly**. The General Assembly makes the state's laws. The **governor** serves as

Georgia State Capital

Georgia's chief executive. The governor is responsible for enforcing state laws. Like the president, he or she may choose to veto laws. He or she also acts as the commander in chief of Georgia's National Guard. The **Georgia Supreme Court** is the state's highest court. State courts make sure Georgia's state and local laws are fair and follow the state constitution.

LOCAL GOVERNMENT

Atlanta Mayor Kasim Reed

City Council Meeting

Local governments are responsible for counties, cities, and towns. **County commissions** (county governments) and **city/town councils** (city/town governments) serve as legislative branches. Citizens usually elect the people who serve on these bodies. Local legislative bodies pass local laws and deal with local policies. **Mayors**, **county managers**, and **city managers** act as local executives. Sometimes citizens directly elect these executives. Sometimes the local legislative branch appoints them.

LEVEL OF GOVERNMENT	*LEGISLATIVE*	*EXECUTIVE*	*JUDICIAL*
State (Georgia)	General Assembly	Governor, Lieutenant Governor, Executive Officials, Boards, and Agencies	state courts, with Georgia Supreme Court serving as the highest in the state
Local	City Council, Town Council, County Commission	Mayor, City / County Manager	local courts fall under the state judicial branch

Practice 3.1: Principles of Republican Government

1. Which of the following people is part of the national legislative branch?

   A. the president

   B. A U.S. Senator from Georgia

   C. a member of the General Assembly

   D. the chief justice

2. The executive branch is responsible for
   A. making laws.

   B. ruling on laws.

   C. enforcing laws.

   D. impeaching officials.

3. Which of the following people is part of an executive branch?
   A. mayor   C. judge

   B. congressman   D. city council member

4. What does "separation of powers" mean? Why did the founders of the United States want a government that included separation of powers?

3.2 CHARACTER TRAITS OF POSITIVE CITIZENSHIP

Character is what makes you the person you are. Your character determines how you act, treat other people, and handle things that happen. Great leaders and citizens have **positive character traits**. A few positive character traits are listed below.

Cooperation	When people cooperate, they work together to solve problems. In chapter 1, we read how the black abolitionist, Frederick Douglass, cooperated with white abolitionists to tell people about the evils of slavery. During the Great Depression, President Roosevelt cooperated with Congress and other leaders to deal with economic challenges. During the 1960s, President Lyndon Johnson cooperated with Congress and civil rights leaders to pass civil rights laws and laws meant to end poverty. Poor migrant farm workers cooperated and worked together under the leadership of Cesar Chavez to win better conditions for laborers. These are just a few historic examples of cooperation.
Diligence	People who are diligent work hard and with great focus. They pursue goals wisely. Women like Susan B. Anthony showed great diligence in the way they organized the women's suffrage movement. They stayed focused and worked hard in the face of great challenges. Their diligence led to women winning the right to vote nationally in 1920.  **Susan B. Anthony**

Liberty	Liberty is the freedom to act and believe the way you want to. Many historical figures became heroes because they defended liberty. In chapter 1, we learned about Thurgood Marshall. Marshall became a hero of the civil rights movement. As a lawyer, he stood up and fought for the liberty of an African American girl to attend an all-white school. Later, as the first African American on the Supreme Court, he continued to stand up for liberty by protecting peoples' rights under the Constitution. **Thurgood Marshall**
Justice	People who value justice seek equal treatment under the law for everyone. Many of the historic figures we studied in chapter 1 valued justice. Eleanor Roosevelt stood up for human rights. Frederick Douglass fought to end slavery. Thurgood Marshall stood up to racism. Lyndon Johnson sought to protect the rights of the poor and minorities. Cesar Chavez fought for justice for migrant workers.
Tolerance	Tolerant people respect others' rights to believe differently. The United States is full of many different kinds of people. Tolerance is important if people hope to get along with one another. **Tolerance**

Freedom of Conscience and Expression	Freedom of conscience means the freedom to think and feel the way you want. Freedom of expression is the freedom to express how you think and feel. People express things in different ways. Some say how they feel through speeches or protests. Some write how they feel or what they believe in newspapers or books. Colonists who favored independence at the time of the American Revolution, women who marched for suffrage, and many other U.S. citizens have exercised freedom of conscience and expression.
Respect for Authority	Authority means being in charge. The federal government has authority over the nation. State governments have authority over states. Teachers have authority over students. And parents have authority over children. People who respect authority accept the authority over them. Sometimes, historical figures have not  **Interacting with Authority** accepted authority. Paul Revere and other supporters of the American Revolution did not accept England's authority over the colonies. Frederick Douglass did not accept slaveholders' authority over African American slaves. Cesar Chavez did not accept the authority of farmers over Hispanic migrant workers. Many historical figures became heroes because they stood up to authorities that they believed were unjust. At other times, historic figures have accepted authority. Thurgood Marshall used the authority of the courts to win rights for African Americans. Franklin Roosevelt used the authority of the federal government to put in place his New Deal.

Practice 3.2: Character Traits of Positive Citizenship

Get with a group of three or four classmates. Make a list of the historical figures studied in chapter 1. For each of these figures, write a brief paragraph describing how he or she shows two or more of the positive character traits discussed in section 3.2. Ask your teacher for help if needed.

CHAPTER 3 REVIEW

Key Terms and People

U.S. Constitution	chief justice	diligence
separation of powers	appeal	liberty
legislative branch	federal government	justice
Congress	state governments	tolerance
House of Representatives	General Assembly	freedom of conscience
Senate	governor	and expression
executive branch	Georgia Supreme Court	respect for authority
president	local governments	
veto	county commissions	
vice president	city and town councils	
cabinet	mayors, county managers, city managers	
judicial branch	cooperation	
United States Supreme Court		

Multiple Choice Questions:

1. Which of the following people is responsible for making laws?

    A. president

    B. chief justice

    C. federal judge

    D. U.S. senator

2. The president of the United States is part of the

   A. legislative branch.

   B. executive branch.

   C. judicial branch.

   D. cabinet.

3. Charlie introduces a new state law against wearing hats in schools. Before Charlie's bill can become a state law, it will have to pass in the

   A. city council.

   B. House of Representatives.

   C. Congress.

   D. General Assembly.

4. Margaret needs to choose a title for the following list. Which title would be the **best**?

   - President
   - Vice President
   - Secretary of State
   - Secretary of Defense

   A. Members of the U.S. Senate

   B. Members of the Judicial Branch

   C. Members of the Executive Branch

   D. Members of the President's Cabinet

5. City councils and county commissions are **best** described as

   A. local legislative branches.

   B. small federal governments.

   C. local executive branches.

   D. state judicial branches.

6. Which of the following would hear an appeal from someone who claims a law violated the Constitution?

   A. Congress

   B. the president

   C. the General Assembly

   D. the Supreme Court

7. Robert believes that the country should have lower taxes. Amber thinks that high taxes are fine, as long as the money is spent to help the poor. Although they disagree, Robert and Amber accept one another as friends and respect one another. This is an example of

   A. diligence.

   B. separation of powers.

   C. tolerance.

   D. justice.

8. When the president and Congress work together to solve the nation's problems, it is an example of

   A. justice.

   B. the cabinet at work.

   C. cooperation.

   D. veto power.

Chapter 4
Economic Understandings

This chapter addresses the following GPS-based CRCT standard(s):

SS3E1	The student will describe the four types of productive resources.
SS3E2	The student will explain that governments provide certain types of goods and services in a market economy and pay for these through taxes and will describe services such as schools, libraries, roads, police/fire protection and military.
SS3E3	The student will give examples of interdependence and trade and will explain how voluntary exchange benefits both parties.
SS3E4	The student will describe the costs and benefits of personal spending and saving choices.

4.1 PRODUCING GOODS AND SERVICES

In this chapter, we will talk about the U.S. **economy**. What businesses sell, what people buy, and how businesses, governments, and people spend their money all affect the economy. On the next page are some important terms to understand when studying the U.S. economy.

Producers	Producers make things. People, businesses, and governments can all be producers.
Consumers	Consumers buy the things producers make. People, businesses, and governments can all be consumers.
Goods	Some producers make goods. Goods are things you can hold. Hats, bikes, cheeseburgers, and cell phones are all goods. **Shopping for Goods**
Services	Some producers provide services. Services are things you pay for but can't hold. When a doctor examines you, he or she is providing a service. When sanitation workers pick up your trash, they are providing a service. **Cell Phones**

RESOURCES FOR PRODUCTION

Resources are things that a person, government, or business has. Resources can be used to produce (make) things. They can also be used to buy things. Money is a resource. In this section, we will study four resources needed to produce things.

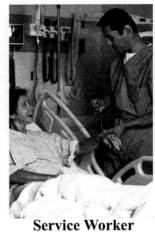

Service Worker

LAND

Land is an important resource. Land includes the natural ground that a person or building stands on. It also includes the buildings themselves. Look at the picture of the factory below. The factory, as well as the land it stands on, is land that is used for production.

LABOR

Labor is the work that people do. Bagging groceries is a form of labor. Fixing cars and typing on a computer are labor as well. Teaching students, answering phones, and the jobs your parents do are all labor. It takes labor to produce things.

Construction Workers

Office Worker

CAPITAL

Capital goods are goods that are used to produce things. Machines in a factory are examples of capital. Trucks that haul things to stores, the computer used to write this book, and staplers used in an office are all capital goods.

Machinery Used for Production

ENTREPRENEURSHIP

S. Truett Cathy

An **entrepreneur** is someone who starts a business. Entrepreneurs raise the money to start a business and decide what the business will produce. Entrepreneurs take great risk. If their business does well, they can make lots of money. If their business does not do well, they could lose money. Entrepreneurs are very important in the U.S. economy. Without entrepreneurs, there would be no businesses.

MARKET ECONOMY

The United States has a market economy. In a **market economy**, price is very important. **Price** is the amount of money consumers pay for goods or services. Producers want to produce things that have a high price. Consumers want to buy things that have a low price.

Producers have to spend money to produce things. They will only sell their goods and services at a price that earns them a profit. **Profit** is the amount of money producers make after paying to produce their good or service. Say that a producer spends $30 to make a shirt. She then sells the same shirt for $100. The producer's profit ($100 – $30) is $70.

Shopping

Consumers will only pay up to a certain price for a good or service. In a market economy, producers sell goods and services at the highest price consumers will pay. If the highest price consumers will pay does not give the producer a profit, then producers will stop producing the good or service.

In some economies, the government sets the prices. The government tells producers what to make. It also tells consumers what they can buy. In a market economy, producers and consumers decide what to produce and buy based on price.

THE GOVERNMENT IN A MARKET ECONOMY

Military

The government provides some goods and services in a market economy. These services are very important, but might not be provided by businesses. The national government provides a military to protect the country. It also provides interstate highways. State governments provide state roads and schools. Local governments provide libraries, police departments, and fire departments. Governments also provide parks and other special services.

Governments need money to pay for the goods and services they provide. They get money in different ways. **Fees** are money that people pay the government to use a good or service. When people in Atlanta pay money to drive on a toll road, they are paying a fee to the government. **Fines** are money people pay the government as punishment for breaking a law. Paying fifty dollars for a speeding ticket is an example of a fine. The number one way the government pays for things is through taxes. **Taxes** are money people and businesses have to pay the government. People have to pay taxes on their income (how much money they make), their homes, and many other things. Businesses have to pay taxes on the profits they make.

Firemen

Library

Practice 4.1:   Producing Goods and Services

1. A business that washes peoples' cars is producing a

    A. good.   B. service.   C. fee.   D. capital good.

2. A warehouse where a business keeps its produced goods is an example of

    A. land.   C. labor.

    B. capital.   D. entrepreneurship.

3. Which of the following is a good or service provided by the government?

    A. running shoes   C. sheriff's department

    B. professional sports   D. fast-food restaurants

4. What is the number-one way governments raise money?

    A. price   B. fees   C. fine   D. taxes

5. Bill makes hats. It costs him $19 to make each hat. He sells each hat for $32 apiece. What are the chances that Bill will keep making and selling hats?

    A. very good

    B. not good

    C. It depends on whether or not Bill can one day make a profit.

    D. One cannot tell based on the information in the question.

4.2 ECONOMIC INTERDEPENDENCE AND PERSONAL MONEY CHOICES

Interdependence means to depend on each other. In the U.S. economy, consumers and producers are interdependent. Consumers depend on producers to make the things. Producers depend on consumers to buy the things. Without producers, consumers would have to make everything they need themselves. Without consumers, producers could not make money.

TRADE

People want or need many things. Some of the things they need are made close to home. People in Georgia can buy many goods that are produced in their home state. Other things are made in different parts of the United States. Some are made in other countries.

Globe

International Trade

When different parts of the country or world sell goods to each other, it is called **trade**. Different areas trade with each other because it is easier than trying to make everything themselves. People in different places are better at producing different things. Certain areas are best at producing farm products. Others are better at making cars or technology. Countries can often buy goods from other nations for less money than producing it at home. Communities, states, and countries trade with one another because it is easier and cheaper. Trade makes different parts of the country and world economically interdependent.

CURRENCY

People use money to buy things. Each country usually has its own currency. **Currency** is anything that is accepted as money. Dollars are currency in the United States. Before countries can trade with one another, they have to know how much the currency in one country is worth in another country. Below is a list of countries and the different currencies they use.

COUNTRY	CURRENCY
United States	Dollar ($)
Great Britain	Pound (£)
Japan	Yen (¥)
Mexico	Peso ($)

PERSONAL SPENDING AND SAVING

Spending Money

When people buy things, they are **spending** money. The good part about spending money is that people get the things they want or need right away. The bad part about spending money is that, after people spend it, the money is gone. They will not be able to buy anything else with that money. If something bad happens, they will not have extra money if they need it.

When people keep their money to use later, they are **saving** money. The bad part about saving money is that people have to do without things they would like to buy. The good part about saving money is that they have the money to buy other things later. If something bad happens, they will have money to spend

Piggy Bank

until things get better. People often save money to buy things that they cannot afford to buy right away. People save money to buy houses, retire from work, or to take a nice trip.

Bank

Practice 4.2: Economic Interdependence and Personal Money Choices

1. Interdependence means to

   A. have your own currency.

   B. save money for later.

   C. depend on each other.

   D. make everything yourself.

2. Why do different states and countries trade with each other?

3. Why do you think it is important to save money?

CHAPTER 4 REVIEW

Key Terms

economy

producers

consumers

goods

services

resources

land

labor

capital goods

entrepreneurship

market economy

price

profit

fees

fines

taxes

interdependence

trade

currency

spending

saving

Multiple Choice Questions

1. Which of the following makes things?

   A. producers

   B. consumers

   C. profits

   D. taxes

2. Which of the following buys things?

   A. producers

   B. consumers

   C. goods

   D. services

3. Land, labor, capital, and entrepreneurship are all needed for

   A. fees.

   B. fines.

   C. production.

   D. resources.

4. Mary Anne saves five hundred dollars for her trip to Japan. Once she gets to Japan, however, she learns that she cannot use dollars to buy things. Mary Anne will have to

   A. find some capital goods.

   B. change her currency.

   C. save more money.

   D. buy services instead of goods.

5. Thomas is a great guitar player and singer. He decides to start his own business. He buys a computer to print fliers and design a web site. Many of the people who learn about Thomas pay him money to play and sing at special events. Read the following four statements. How many of them are true?

   - Thomas is an entrepreneur.
   - Thomas' guitar is land.
   - Thomas' computer is capital.
   - The money Thomas spent on fliers is his profit.

   A. one

   B. two

   C. three

   D. four

6. Which of the following would taxes **most likely** pay for?

    A. a printer at a bank

    B. a bigger factory for a shoe company

    C. a new police car

    D. a computer for a real estate agent

7. Farmers in Georgia sell peanuts to people in New York and Canada. This is called

    A. labor.

    B. capital.

    C. trade.

    D. currency.

8. Brant wants to buy a new house. The house he wants costs $150,000. Brant has $5,000 and only makes $4,000 on his monthly paycheck. To get the house he wants, what will Brant have to do for now?

    A. spend

    B. save

    C. consume

    D. trade

Georgia 3 Social Studies
Practice Test 1

The purpose of this practice test is to measure your progress in Social Studies. This test is based on the GPS-based Georgia CRCT in Social Studies and adheres to the sample question format provided by the Georgia Department of Education.

General Directions:

1. Read all directions carefully.

2. Read each question or sample. Then, choose the best answer.

3. Choose only one answer for each question. If you change an answer, be sure to erase your original answer completely.

1. Greek architecture is also called

   A. democracy.

   B. Draco.

   C. representative.

   D. classical.

   SS3H1

2. Who is **best** known as a leader of the women's suffrage movement?

   A. Mary McLeod Bethune

   B. Eleanor Roosevelt

   C. Cesar Chavez

   D. Susan B. Anthony

   SS3H2

3. A positive character trait of good leaders is

   A. honesty

   B. fear.

   C. selfishness.

   D. none of the above.

   SS3CG2

4. Which of the following is **true?**

   A. Producers want to produce things that have a low price.

   B. Consumers want to buy things that have a low price.

   C. Producers do not have to spend money to produce things.

   D. Consumers will always pay high prices for goods.

   SS3E3

5. The study of the earth is called

   A. history.

   B. latitude.

   C. geography.

   D. meridian.

   SS3G1

6. The Constitution is the

   A. branch of government that enforces laws.

   B. national set of U.S. laws.

   C. legislative branch of Georgia.

   D. state's lowest court.

   SS3CG1

7. Which of the following buys things?   SS3E1
   A. producers   C. goods

   B. consumers   D. services

8. Every four years, athletes from all over the world compete in a   SS3H1
   famous sporting event. What is this event called?
   A. United Nations

   B. the suffrage movement

   C. the Olympics

   D. a direct democracy

9. What would be the **best** title for the list below?   SS3H2
   • Franklin Roosevelt

   • Susan B. Anthony

   • Mary McLeod Bethune

   A. People Who Impacted the American Revolution

   B. Leaders of the Abolitionist Movement

   C. Famous U.S. Senators

   D. People Who Have Impacted U.S. Democracy

10. The river that runs from Minnesota to the Gulf of Mexico is the   SS3G1
    A. Hudson.   C. Colorado.

    B. Mississippi.   D. Rio Grande.

11. The president is the   SS3CG1
    A. head of the judicial branch.

    B. leader of the Senate.

    C. head of the executive branch.

    D. head of the Supreme Court.

12. Which of the following is provided by the government? SS3E2

    A. restaurants

    B. car repair shops

    C. libraries

    D. music stores

13. Frederick Douglass worked with white abolitionists to tell peo- SS3CG2
    ple about the evils of slavery. This is an example of

    A. cooperation.

    B. dishonesty.

    C. racism.

    D. separation of powers.

14. Jack spends $5 on a comic book, and he sells it for $10. He SS3E3
    makes $5. The $5 Jack makes is called

    A. fine.   C. resource.

    B. profit.   D. payment.

15. How did Franklin Roosevelt try to help the United States during SS3H2
    the 1930s?

    A. He provided a program called the New Deal.

    B. He led the country through World War II.

    C. He fought for migrant workers.

    D. He helped end slavery.

16. The United States is SS3H1

    A. a direct democracy.

    B. a representative democracy.

    C. not a democracy.

    D. an Athenian democracy.

Use the map below to answer question number 17.

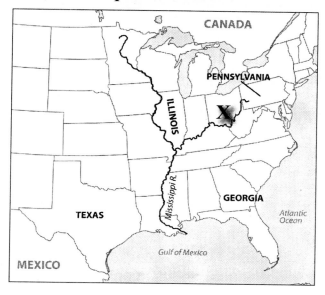

17. What does the X on the map represent?   SS3G1
    A. the Grand Canyon

    B. the Colorado River

    C. the Ohio River

    D. the Rocky Mountains

18. The Constitution established three branches of government.   SS3CG1
    What is this called?
    A. separation of powers

    B. diligence

    C. General Assembly

    D. Bill of Rights

19. The number-one way the government raises money is through   SS3E2
    A. taxes.

    B. fines.

    C. fees.

    D. prices.

20. Michelle is making an outline for a school report. What should   SS3E1
    go where the question mark is?
    A. Capital Goods

        1. Machines in a factory

        2. Staplers in an office

        3.   ?

    A. The government raising taxes

    B. Trucks used to haul things to stores

    C. Police officers going to work

    D. Grocery workers bagging groceries

21. The United States Supreme Court building is an example of   SS3H1
    A. a direct democracy.

    B. Draco's system of lawmaking.

    C. Greek architecture's impact on the United States.

    D. a representative democracy.

22. Lyndon B. Johnson   SS3H2
    A. wanted to make America the "Great Society."

    B. was the first African American Supreme Court judge.

    C. helped win rights for migrant farm workers.

    D. led the United States through World War II.

23. The freedom to act and believe the way you want to is called   SS3CG2
    A. a responsibility.

    B. liberty.

    C. cooperation.

    D. authority.

Use the map below to answer the question number 24.

24. What does the image above **most likely** represent?   SS3G1

   A. Rocky Mountains

   B. Colorado River

   C. Northwest Territory

   D. Appalachian Mountains

25. Money that people pay the government in order to use a good or   SS3E2
    service is called a

   A. fine.   C. good.

   B. fee.   D. profit.

26. How did Cesar Chavez show his belief in liberty?   SS3CG2

   A. He did not display liberty.

   B. by fighting for better rights for migrant workers

   C. by fighting for the rights of African Americans

   D. by running for president of the United States

27. Who became a United Nations delegate?   SS3H2
    A. Frederick Douglass

    B. Cesar Chavez

    C. Eleanor Roosevelt

    D. Susan B. Anthony

28. Which river runs through New York?   SS3G1
    A. Hudson   C. Mississippi

    B. Rio Grande   D. Appalachian

29. Melanie votes for Ben who will make decisions for her in   SS3H1
    Congress. What is this an example of?
    A. direct democracy

    B. representative democracy

    C. Greek architecture

    D. human rights

30. What happens to a bill if the president does not sign it?   SS3CG1
    A. It does not become a law unless two-thirds of each house vote in favor
       of the bill again.

    B. It never becomes a law.

    C. It only becomes a law if a majority of each house votes in favor of the
       bill again.

    D. It becomes a law anyway since the majority of Congress voted for it.

31. Two types of resources are   SS3E1
    A. goods and services.

    B. consumers and producers.

    C. land and labor.

    D. price and profit.

32. The list below needs a title. What would be the **best** title? SS3H1
    - architecture
    - the Olympics
    - democracy
    A. Greek Influences on the United States

    B. American Influences on Greece

    C. Ideas of Paul Revere

    D. Roosevelt's New Deal

33. Jack and Tracy support different candidates for president. Even SS3CG2
    though they have different views, they remain friends. This is an
    example of

    A. respecting authority.

    B. tolerance.

    C. liberty.

    D. selfishness.

He escaped to the North and became free. He was a powerful speaker who fought for the civil rights of slaves. He is often called the founder of the American civil rights movement.

34. Who is the statement above describing? SS3H2
    A. Cesar Chavez

    B. Paul Revere

    C. Frederick Douglass

    D. Lyndon B. Johnson

35. The work that people do is called SS3E1
    A. land.   C. capital goods.

    B. labor.   D. price.

Use the map below to answer question number 36.

36. What does the image represent?   SS3G1

    A. Ohio River

    B. Rio Grande River

    C. Grand Canyon

    D. Appalachian Mountains

37. When people buy things, they are   SS3E4

    A. saving their money.

    B. making a profit.

    C. entrepreneurs.

    D. spending their money.

38. Your school probably has children of different races. Who is   SS3H2
most remembered for helping to make sure that children of
different races can go to the same school?

    A. Thurgood Marshall

    B. Cesar Chavez

    C. Frederick Douglass

    D. Franklin Roosevelt

Use the images below to answer questions 39, 40, 41, and 42.

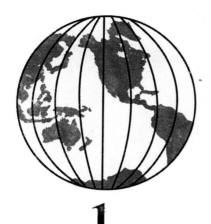

1

2

39. Which image shows meridians?   SS3G1
    A. 1   C. both

    B. 2   D. neither

40. Which image separates the world into hemispheres?   SS3G1
    A. 1   C. both

    B. 2   D. neither

41. Which image shows parallels?   SS3G1
    A. 1   C. both

    B. 2   D. neither

42. On which image would one find the equator labeled?   SS3G1
    A. 1   C. both

    B. 2   D. neither

43. The executive branch of the national government is responsible for   SS3CG1

 A. making sure that people follow the laws.

 B. creating the laws.

 C. making sure laws are fair and constitutional.

 D. state laws.

44. How did Thurgood Marshall show respect for authority?   SS3CG2

 A. He protested poor working conditions to win rights for migrant workers.

 B. He did not show any respect for authority.

 C. He went through the federal government to gain rights for women.

 D. He went through the courts to win rights for African Americans.

45. Which of the following makes things?   SS3E1

 A. producers   C. profits

 B. consumers   D. prices

46. Greece's first constitution was written by   SS3H1

 A. Draco.

 B. the citizens.

 C. Cesar Chavez.

 D. Greece didn't have a constitution.

47. Farmers in Idaho sell potatoes to people in Boston and New York. This is called   SS3E3

 A. capital.

 B. trade.

 C. labor.

 D. currency.

48. Money people pay the government as punishment for breaking   SS3E2
    the law is called a

    A. tax.   C. capital good.

    B. service.   D. fine.

49. Who is the following list describing?   SS3H2

   • Supported the American Revolution

   • Famous picture of Boston Massacre

   • Midnight ride

    A. Frederick Douglass

    B. Paul Revere

    C. Thurgood Marshall

    D. Lyndon B. Johnson

Read the passage below to answer the following question.

It is a tributary of the Mississippi River. It runs from Pennsylvania to Illinois. During colonial times, it served as a boundary between the British colonies and Native American territory.

50. What is the passage above referring to?   SS3G1

    A. Hudson River

    B. Ohio River

    C. Rio Grande River

    D. Colorado River

51. Which branch of government is responsible for making laws?   SS3CG1

    A. legislative

    B. executive

    C. judicial

    D. the president

52. Which of the following people is part of a state government?   SS3CG1

    A. governor

    B. chief justice

    C. vice president

    D. congressman

53. Who is best known for starting a school for African American   SS3H2
    students?

    A. Mary McLeod Bethune

    B. Eleanor Roosevelt

    C. Cesar Chavez

    D. Susan B. Anthony

54. When a doctor examines you, he is providing a   SS3E1
    A. fee.   C. service.

    B. good.   D. capital good.

55. Jackie is making an outline for a school report. What should go   SS3H1
    where the question mark is?

    A. Representative Democracy

        1.   ?

        2. People elect representatives to vote on issues and policies for them.

    A. Olympic Games

    B. Athens, Greece

    C. United States

    D. the Parthenon

56. Which of the following is **true**?   SS3G1

    A. The Appalachian Mountains are in New Mexico.

    B. The Rocky Mountains are in the western United States.

    C. The Rio Grande separates New York from Canada.

    D. The Ohio River separates eastern and western United States.

57. The parallel line that runs around a globe at its center is the   SS3G1

    A. meridian.

    B. hemisphere.

    C. equator.

    D. International Date Line.

58. What do the president, vice president, and the cabinet have in   SS3CG1
    common?

    A. They have nothing in common.

    B. They are part of Congress.

    C. They are part of the judicial branch.

    D. They are part of the executive branch.

59. How did Paul Revere protect democracy and freedom?   SS3H2

    A. by taking part in the New Deal

    B. by supporting the American Revolution

    C. by running for president of the United States

    D. by helping migrant workers

60. Mr. Turner opens up his own landscaping business. This is an   SS3E1
    example of

    A. entrepreneurship.   C. a capital good.

    B. paying taxes.   D. trade.

61. Who helped win more rights for migrant farm workers?   SS3H2

    A. Lyndon B. Johnson

    B. Franklin Roosevelt

    C. Cesar Chavez

    D. Thurgood Marshall

62. Meridians are   SS3G1

    A. lines of latitude.

    B. only found in the western hemisphere.

    C. lines that run east and west.

    D. lines of longitude.

63. Which branch of government is responsible for making sure laws are fair and constitutional?   SS3CG1

    A. legislative   C. judicial

    B. executive   D. assembly

64. Ben thinks that all people have rights, no matter what country they live in. Who of the following clearly shared Ben's view?   SS3H2

    A. the Parthenon

    B. Frederick Douglass

    C. Eleanor Roosevelt

    D. Lyndon Johnson

65. Georgia's chief executive is the   SS3CG1

    A. governor.

    B. chief justice.

    C. vice president.

    D. mayor.

66. Look at the drawing below. What should go where the question SS3CG1
mark below is?

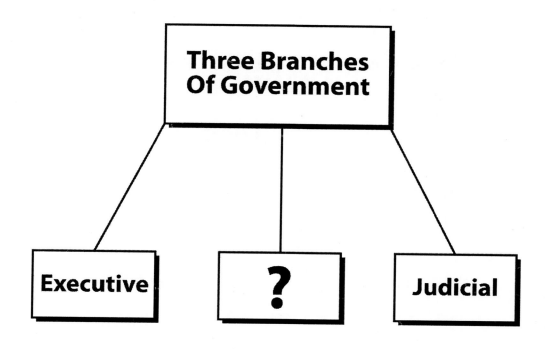

A. state

B. legislative

C. federal

D. national

67. The Voting Rights Act of 1965 SS3H2

A. made it possible for women to vote.

B. made it easier for African Americans to vote.

C. would not let poor migrant farmers vote.

D. was created by Paul Revere.

68. The national government is also called the SS3CG1

A. federal government.

B. Congress.

C. General Assembly.

D. administration.

69. Which of the following people is part of the national legislative   SS3CG1
branch of government?

A. the president

B. the chief justice

C. a U.S. Senator

D. a city council member

70. Which branch of government has the power to impeach the   SS3CG1
president?

A. state governments

B. the legislative

C. the executive

D. the judicial

Georgia 3 Social Studies
Practice Test 2

The purpose of this practice test is to measure your progress in Social Studies. This test is based on the GPS-based Georgia CRCT in Social Studies and adheres to the sample question format provided by the Georgia Department of Education.

General Directions:

1. Read all directions carefully.

2. Read each question or sample. Then, choose the best answer.

3. Choose only one answer for each question. If you change an answer, be sure to erase your original answer completely.

1. Which statement is **true**?   SS3H1

    A. Classical architecture made the Greeks seem weak.

    B. Classical architecture made the Greeks seem powerful.

    C. The Greeks did not use classical architecture.

    D. Classical architecture made the Greeks seem violent.

2. Susan B. Anthony was a   SS3H2

    A. strong supporter of women's rights.

    B. leader in the abolitionist movement.

    C. migrant farm worker.

    D. lawyer who fought for civil rights.

3. Cooperation, diligence, liberty, and justice are   SS3CG2

    A. positive character traits of citizens.

    B. natural rights.

    C. reasons people become political leaders.

    D. forms of expression.

4. The amount of money consumers pay for goods and services is   SS3E3
   called

    A. profit.   C. price.

    B. taxes.   D. labor.

5. Which United States document establishes the nation's laws?   SS3CG1

    A. the General Assembly   C. the Bill of Rights

    B. the Constitution   D. the U.S. Cabinet

6. Jennifer goes to the mall and buys a new shirt. Jennifer is   SS3E1

    A. an entrepreneur.   C. a consumer.

    B. a producer.   D. an employee

7. The ancient Greeks held the first   SS3H1

   A. presidential election.

   B. Olympic Games.

   C. civil rights court case.

   D. representative democracy.

8. Which river allows people to travel between the Gulf of Mexico   SS3G1
and the central United States?

   A. Mississippi   C. Colorado

   B. Hudson   D. Rio Grande

9. Which of the following is provided by the government?   SS3E2

   A. schools

   B. hiking shoes

   C. gas stations

   D. hair salons

Read the statement below.

> It must approve treaties with other countries and public officials appointed by the president. It also has the power to impeach the president and other public officials.

10. What is the statement describing?   SS3CG1

   A. powers of the executive branch

   B. powers of the legislative branch

   C. powers of the judicial branch.

   D. powers of the General Assembly

11. During the Great Depression, President Roosevelt worked with Congress to deal with economic challenges. This is an example of

SS3CG2

A. justice.

B. separation of powers.

C. cooperation.

D. the cabinet at work.

12. Mary McLeod Bethune

SS3H2

A. helped slaves escape North.

B. warned colonists that the British were coming during the Revolution.

C. started a school for African Americans.

D. created the New Deal to help the U.S. economy.

13. An important part of Greek architecture was the use of

SS3H1

A. columns.   C. timber.

B. tables.   D. poles.

14. Instead of giving all the governing power to one leader, the Constitution establishes three branches of government. This is called

SS3CG1

A. the U.S. Cabinet.

B. the General Assembly.

C. separation of powers.

D. compromise.

15. Which river runs from Pennsylvania to Illinois?

SS3G1

A. Ohio

B. Hudson

C. Rio Grande

D. Colorado

Use the picture below to answer question 16.

16. Who is this a picture of?   SS3H2

   A. Paul Revere

   B. Draco

   C. Cesar Chavez

   D. Franklin Roosevelt

17. How did Cesar Chavez adapt to his surroundings?   SS3G2

   A. He helped win better rights for migrant workers.

   B. He worked to end poverty in the United States.

   C. He was the first African American judge on the Supreme Court.

   D. He started a school for African American students.

18. How did Mary McLeod Bethune display liberty?   SS3CG2

    A. by supporting the American Revolution

    B. by becoming the first woman lawyer

    C. by starting a school for African American students

    D. by escaping from slavery

19. A computer was used to write these questions. The computer is   SS3E1
    an example of

    A. a profit.

    B. labor.

    C. currency.

    D. a capital good.

20. Taxes are   SS3E2

    A. important services provided by the government.

    B. money people and businesses have to pay the government.

    C. the amount of money consumers pay for goods or services.

    D. the amount of money a producer makes.

21. The United States Supreme Court building was **most** influenced   SS3H1
    by

    A. the Parthenon.

    B. Draco's laws.

    C. the Olympic Games.

    D. Paul Revere.

22. Lines of latitude are called   SS3G1
    A. International Lines.   C. meridians.

    B. parallels.   D. equators.

23. In 2008, Barack Obama became the first African American ever   SS3H2
    nominated for president. Who helped pass laws that made it
    easier for African Americans to run for president?
    A. Lyndon B. Johnson

    B. Paul Revere

    C. Cesar Chavez

    D. Susan B. Anthony

24. The Appalachian Mountains are located in the   SS3G1
    A. western United States.

    B. eastern United States.

    C. Gulf of Mexico.

    D. Northwest Territory.

25. Look at the drawing below. What should go in the last circle   SS3CG1
    where the question mark is?

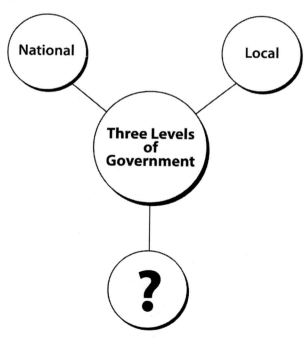

    A. federal   C. judicial

    B. state   D. county

26. Interstate highways and military defense are provided by   SS3E2

    A. the government.

    B. consumers.

    C. entrepreneurs.

    D. businesses.

27. Who is the following list describing?   SS3H2

    • President of the United States
    • Created the New Deal
    • Led the country through World War II

    A. Lyndon B. Johnson

    B. Franklin Roosevelt

    C. Frederick Douglass

    D. Cesar Chavez

28. Which river meets the Atlantic Ocean at New York City?   SS3G1

    A. Rio Grande   C. Hudson

    B. Mississippi   D. Colorado

29. Which of the following is an example of a representative democracy?   SS3H1

    A. Kelly does not get to vote in any elections.

    B. Tanya refuses to obey the law.

    C. Brian votes for Heather who will make decisions for him in Congress.

    D. Every citizen gets to vote on every issue that comes before Congress.

30. The leader of the Senate is the   SS3CG1

    A. mayor.   C. president.

    B. vice president.   D. governor.

31. Interdependence means to SS3E3
    A. make your own money.

    B. save a lot of money

    C. depend on each other.

    D. pay taxes.

32. Land, labor, capital, and entrepreneurship are all important for SS3E1
    A. saving money.   C. fees.

    B. production.   D. fines.

33. The United States and ancient Greece are different because SS3H1
    A. the U.S. is a direct democracy, but Greece was a representative democracy.

    B. the U.S. is a representative democracy, but Greece was a direct democracy.

    C. the U.S. and Greece have no differences.

    D. the U.S. has a constitution, but Greece did not have any written laws.

34. Susan B. Anthony worked hard to help the women's suffrage SS3CG2
    movement. She was focused and persistent. This is an example of
    A. diligence.

    B. veto power.

    C. separation of powers.

    D. selfishness.

35. Tom is a black male. He lives in the South in 1842. Who of the SS3H2
    following would have fought for Tom's rights?
    A. Cesar Chavez   C. Frederick Douglass

    B. Paul Revere   D. Lyndon B. Johnson

36. Texas is separated from Mexico by the   SS3G1
   A. Appalachian Mountains

   B. Colorado River.

   C. Rocky Mountains

   D. Rio Grande River.

37. Rebecca wants to buy a new car. The car she wants costs $8000. SS3E4
   Rebecca has $1000 and only makes $3000 on her monthly pay-
   check. To get the car she wants, what will Rebecca have to do for now?
   A. trade   C. save

   B. consume   D. spend

38. Thurgood Marshall was   SS3H2
   A. a Mexican American farm worker.

   B. a lawyer who fought for the rights of African Americans.

   C. president of the United States from 1963 – 1969.

   D. a leader during World War II.

39. Eleanor Roosevelt actively supported   SS3H2
   A. the American Revolution.

   B. human rights.

   C. slavery.

   D. World War I.

40. When your mom drives a car in Georgia, she has to wear a seat- SS3H1
   belt. This is an example of a
   A. constitution.

   B. punishment.

   C. democracy.

   D. law.

Use this map to answer question number 41.

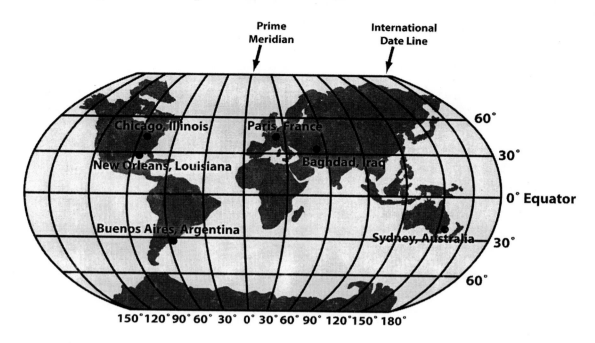

41. Which city is located closest to 35° N, 44° E?   SS3G1

    A. Chicago   C. Baghdad

    B. Paris   D. Sydney

42. John McCain and Barack Obama are running for president. The   SS3CG1
    winner will become part of the

    A. judicial branch.

    B. executive branch.

    C. legislative branch.

    D. Senate.

43. Jack makes hats. He sells the hats for seven dollars each. Jack is a   SS3E1
    A. consumer.

    B. government worker.

    C. producer.

    D. teacher.

44. The United States Senate has   SS3CG1

    A. one Senator from each state.

    B. two Senators from each state.

    C. three Senators from each state.

    D. It depends on the population of the state.

45. Brian saves three hundred dollars for his trip to Great Britain.   SS3E3
    Once he gets to Great Britain, he learns that he cannot use dollars
    to buy things. Brian will have to

    A. change his currency.

    B. save extra money.

    C. buy services instead of goods.

    D. become an entrepreneur.

46. If someone gets a speeding ticket, they often have to pay a   SS3E2
    A. tax.   C. fine.

    B. service.   D. price.

47. The longest river in the United States is the   SS3G1

    A. Ohio River.

    B. Missouri River.

    C. Rio Grande River.

    D. Colorado River.

48. In Ancient Greece, all adult males over the age of eighteen could   SS3H1
    vote on issues. What is this an example of?

    A. direct democracy

    B. representative democracy

    C. Draco's democracy

    D. the constitution

49. The legislative branch of government is responsible for
    A. making sure people follow the laws. SS3CG1
    B. making the laws.
    C. making sure laws are fair and constitutional.
    D. appointing members of the Supreme Court.

50. In Georgia, the legislative branch of government is the SS3CG1
    A. National Guard.
    B. Attorney General.
    C. General Assembly.
    D. Supreme Court.

51. Who is the list below describing? SS3H2
    • educator
    • civil rights leader
    • started a school for African Americans
    • became one of Roosevelt's advisors
    A. Mary McLeod Bethune
    B. Cesar Chavez
    C. Susan B. Anthony
    D. Lyndon B. Johnson

52. When you get your haircut, the salon is providing a SS3E1
    A. fee.
    B. good.
    C. service.
    D. capital good.

53. The Rocky Mountains are   SS3G1

    A. in the western United States.

    B. in the eastern United States.

    C. located in Georgia and Tennessee.

    D. found in the Gulf of Mexico.

54. The equator is the   SS3G1

    A. northern half of the world.

    B. parallel line that runs around the earth at its center.

    C. meridian located at 180 degrees longitude.

    D. line that runs north and south on a globe.

55. How many representatives does each state have in the House of   SS3CG1
    Representatives?

    A. one

    B. two

    C. three

    D. It depends on the population of the state.

56. Franklin Roosevelt   SS3H1

    A. helped slaves escape North.

    B. warned colonists that the British were coming during the Revolution.

    C. started a school for African Americans.

    D. created the New Deal to help the U.S. economy.

57. Which of the following people is responsible for making laws?   SS3CG1
    A. chief justice   C. U.S. Senator

    B. president   D. federal judge

58. If your dad started his own business, he would be known as   SS3E1

    A. a capital good.

    B. a profit.

    C. a consumer.

    D. an entrepreneur.

59. Don is a mechanic. He works on cars everyday. Don's work is an   SS3E1
    example of

    A. capital goods.   C. profit.

    B. labor.   D. price.

60. Cesar Chavez   SS3H2

    A. led Mexican American farm workers.

    B. made it possible for women to vote.

    C. was the first African American Supreme Court judge.

    D. started a school for African Americans.

61. The Grand Canyon was created by the   SS3G1

    A. Ohio River.

    B. Rocky Mountains.

    C. Colorado River.

    D. Rio Grande River.

62. Lines that run north–south on a map are called   SS3G1

    A. meridians.

    B. parallels.

    C. equators.

    D. International Date Lines.

63. Which branch of government is responsible for making sure laws do not violate the rights of citizens?   SS3CG1
    A. legislative   C. judicial
    B. executive   D. the Senate

64. What did Franklin Roosevelt create to help the economy?   SS3H2
    A. the United Nations
    B. the Parthenon
    C. the New Deal
    D. He did not create anything to help the economy.

65. The second-highest executive in the United States is the   SS3CG1
    A. governor.   C. vice president.
    B. Senate.   D. chief justice.

66. Lines that run east–west on a map are called   SS3G1
    A. meridians.
    B. parallels.
    C. equators.
    D. International Date Lines.

67. Which of the following is **true?**   SS3H2
    A. Frederick Douglass lived in fear of being returned as a slave to the South.
    B. Frederick Douglass could have been arrested and hanged for taking part in the Revolution.
    C. Frederick Douglass was often threatened by migrant farm workers.
    D. Frederick Douglass was often ignored as he spoke about the "Great Society."

68. Jim needs to choose a title for the following list. Which title would be the **best**?   SS3CG1

   • Congress

   • the president

   • the federal courts

   A. The Federal Government

   B. The General Assembly

   C. The President's Cabinet

   D. The Supreme Court

69. Which of the following people is part of a local executive branch?

   A. county commissioner   SS3CG1

   B. mayor

   C. judge

   D. senator

70. Local governments are responsible for   SS3CG1

   A. national laws.

   B. state highways.

   C. international agreements.

   D. city speed limits.

American Book Company
The Standards Experts

MASTERING THE GEORGIA

3RD GRADE CRCT

IN

Social Studies

ANSWER KEY
2008

American Book Company
PO Box 2638
Woodstock, GA 30188-1383
Toll Free Phone: 1-888-264-5877   Toll Free Fax: 1-866-827-3240
Web site: www.americanbookcompany.com

Georgia 3 CRCT Social Studies Standards Chart

<table>
<tr><td colspan="4"> Georgia 3 CRCT Social Studies Chart of Standards The following chart correlates each question on the Diagnostic Test, Practice Test 1, and Practice Test 2 to the Georgia 7 CRCT competency goals standards and benchmarks published by the Georgia Department of Education. These test questions are also correlated with chapters in Georgia 4 CRCT Social Studies.</td></tr>
<tr><td>Chapter Number</td><td>Diagnostic Test Questions</td><td>Practice Test 1 Questions</td><td>Practice Test 2 Questions</td></tr>
<tr><td colspan="4">Historical Understandings</td></tr>
<tr><td colspan="4">SS3H1 The student will explain the political roots of our modern democracy in the United States of America.

a. Identify the influence of Greek architecture (Parthenon, U.S. Supreme Court building), law, and the Olympic Games on the present.

b. Explain the ancient Athenians' idea that a community should choose its own leaders.

c. Compare and contrast Athens as a direct democracy with the United States as a representative democracy.</td></tr>
<tr><td>1</td><td>1, 9, 21, 25, 32, 33, 42, 46, 52</td><td>1, 8, 16, 21, 29, 32, 46, 55</td><td>1, 7, 13, 21, 29, 33, 40, 48, 56</td></tr>
<tr><td colspan="4">SS3H2 The student will discuss the lives of Americans who expanded people's rights and freedoms in a democracy.

a. Paul Revere (independence), Frederick Douglass (civil rights), Susan B. Anthony (women's rights), Mary McLeod Bethune (education), Franklin D. Roosevelt (New Deal and World War II), Eleanor Roosevelt (United Nations and human rights), Thurgood Marshall (civil rights), Lyndon B. Johnson (Great Society and voting rights), and Cesar Chavez (workers' rights).

b. Explain social barriers, restrictions, and obstacles that these historical figures had to overcome and describe how they overcame them.</td></tr>
<tr><td>1</td><td>2, 10, 16, 26, 30, 40, 47, 51, 58, 63, 65, 69</td><td>2, 9, 15, 22, 27, 34, 38, 49, 53, 59, 61, 64, 67</td><td>2, 12, 16, 23, 27, 35, 38, 39, 51, 60, 64, 67</td></tr>
</table>

Chapter Number	Diagnostic Test Questions	Practice Test 1 Questions	Practice Test 2 Questions
Geographic Understandings			
SS3G1 The student will locate major topographical features of the United States of America.			
a. Identify major rivers of the United States of America: Mississippi, Ohio, Rio Grande, Colorado, Hudson.			
b. Identify major mountain ranges of the United States of America: Appalachian, Rocky.			
c. Locate the equator, prime meridian, and lines of latitude and longitude on a globe.			
d. Locate Greece on a world map.			
2	5, 18, 19, 20, 27, 31, 38, 43, 48, 54, 55, 60, 61, 66	5, 10, 17, 24, 28, 36, 39, 40, 41, 42, 50, 56, 57, 62	8, 15, 22, 24, 28, 36, 41, 47, 53, 54, 61, 62, 66
SS3G2 The student will describe the cultural and geographic systems associated with the historical figures in SS3H2a.			
a. Identify on a political map specific locations significant to the life and times of these historic figures.			
b. Describe how place (physical and human characteristics) had an impact on the lives of these historic figures.			
c. Describe how each of these historic figures adapted to and was influenced by his/her environment.			
d. Trace examples of travel and movement of these historic figures and their ideas across time.			
e. Describe how the region in which these historic figures lived affected their lives and had an impact on their cultural identification.			
2	8	3	17
Government/Civic Understandings			
SS3CG1 The student will explain the importance of the basic principles that provide the foundation of a republican form of government.			
a. Explain why in the United States there is a separation of power between branches of government and levels of government.			
b. Name the three levels of government (national, state, local) and the three branches in each (executive, legislative, judicial), including the names of the legislative branch (Congress, General Assembly, city commission, or city council.			
c. State an example of the responsibilities of each level and branch of government.			
3	6, 11, 17, 22, 28, 34, 45, 49, 50, 57, 62, 64, 67, 68, 70	6, 11, 18, 30, 43, 51, 52, 58, 63, 65, 66, 68, 69, 70	5, 10, 14, 25, 30, 42, 44, 49, 50, 55, 57, 63, 65, 68, 69, 70
SS3CG2 The student will describe how the historical figures in SS3H2a display positive character traits of cooperation, diligence, liberty, justice, tolerance, freedom of conscience and expression, and respect for and acceptance of authority.			
3	3, 13, 23, 37	13, 23, 26, 33, 44	3, 11, 18, 34

Chapter Number	Diagnostic Test Questions	Practice Test 1 Questions	Practice Test 2 Questions
Economic Understandings			

SS3E1 The student will describe the four types of productive resources:
     a. Natural (land)
     b. Human (labor)
     c. Capital (capital goods)
     d. Entrepreneurship (used to create goods and services)			

4	7, 15, 24, 36, 44, 53, 59	7, 20, 31, 35, 45, 54, 60	6, 19, 32, 43, 52, 58, 59
SS3E2 The student will explain that governments provide certain types of goods and services in a market economy and pay for these through taxes and will describe services such as schools, libraries, roads, police/fire protection, and military.			
4	12, 29, 41, 56	12, 19, 25, 48	9, 20, 26, 46

SS3E3 The student will give examples of interdependence and trade and will explain how voluntary exchange benefits both parties.
     a. Describe the interdependence of consumers and producers of goods and services.
     b. Describe how goods and services are allocated by price in the marketplace.
     c. Explain that some things are made locally, some elsewhere in the country, and some in other countries.
     d. Explain that most countries create their own currency for use as money.			

4	4, 14, 35	4, 14, 47	4, 31, 45
SS3E4 The student will describe the costs and benefits of personal spending and saving choices.			
4	39	37	37

Diagnostic Test

Pages 1 – 18

1. C	11. B	21. A	31. D	41. C	51. C	61. C
2. D	12. B	22. D	32. C	42. D	52. B	62. C
3. C	13. C	23. C	33. D	43. C	53. D	63. D
4. C	14. D	24. C	34. B	44. D	54. C	64. C
5. C	15. C	25. C	35. A	45. B	55. B	65. B
6. D	16. A	26. C	36. B	46. D	56. D	66. A
7. A	17. B	27. B	37. B	47. B	57. B	67. B
8. C	18. C	28. C	38. B	48. D	58. C	68. C
9. B	19. C	29. B	39. B	49. C	59. C	69. B
10. D	20. C	30. C	40. A	50. C	60. B	70. C

CHAPTER 1: HISTORICAL UNDERSTANDINGS OF U.S. DEMOCRACY

Practice 1.1: The Impact of Ancient Greece on the United States

Pages 22–23

1. C   2. B   3. D

Practice 1.2: People Who Have Impacted U.S. Democracy

Page 28

1. C

2. 4 Eleanor Roosevelt   5 Franklin Roosevelt
    1 Cesar Chavez   2 Susan B. Anthony
    3 Lyndon Johnson

3. Paul Revere could have been arrested and hanged for taking part in the revolution. Frederick Douglass lived in fear of being captured and returned to slave owners in the South. Mary McLeod Bethune encouraged African Americans to register to vote. She was often threatened by members of the Ku Klux Klan. (The Ku Klux Klan supported violence and hatred for African Americans.) In the beginning, Susan B. Anthony was often ignored as she spoke about women's rights.

Chapter 1 Review

Pages 29–30

Key Terms, People, and Concepts

architecture – the way buildings are built and designed. The ancient Greeks invented classical architecture. Classical architecture made the Greeks seem powerful and impressive. The United States used some elements of classical architecture when designing important buildings like the Supreme Court building.

columns – large poles that support buildings. Classical columns stood at the front entrances of Greek buildings, making the buildings look magnificent.

Parthenon – the most famous example of Greek architecture. The ancient Greeks built the Parthenon as a temple between 447 and 432 BC.

Olympic Games – a series of sporting events. The games began in 776 BC in Olympia, Greece. These games were held until AD 393. The modern Olympic Games began in 1896. Athletes from all over the world gather every four years to compete in both summer and winter games.

democracy – a government ruled by the people. Citizens vote to make decisions. One of the world's first democracies began in Athens, Greece, around 500 BC.

direct democracy – any qualified citizen may vote directly on each law and policy. Athens was a direct democracy. Free adult males over the age of eighteen could vote in Athens. The ancient Greeks called this type of government Athenian democracy. They believed that each community should choose its own leaders and set its own rules.

representative democracy – people elect representatives to vote on issues and policies for them. The United States is a representative democracy. The United States used the ancient ideas of the Greeks to create its own democratic government.

laws – rules set by the government. In 629 BC, a leader named Draco wrote Greece's first constitution. His laws could be read by all citizens. People could finally know what the law said and how to punish those who broke the law.

1

constitution – a written set of laws.

United States Constitution – The Constitution limits the powers of the government by stating what it can, and cannot, do. It also protects people's rights. Like Draco's laws, the U.S. Constitution gives people a written code to live by. U.S. states also have state constitutions. State constitutions are also based on Draco's idea that it is important to have written laws.

Paul Revere – lived at the time of the American Revolution. He wanted the colonies to be independent of Great Britain. Like many, Revere wanted the colonists to form their own country. He made a famous engraving of the Boston Massacre that led many other colonists to want independence too. When the revolution finally started, Revere and other messengers rode their horses through the night to warn colonists that the British were coming. Revere is most remembered for this midnight ride.

Frederick Douglass – an African American who lived during the 1800s. He was an important civil rights activist. Douglass grew up as a slave in the South. As an adult, he escaped to the North and became free. Douglass educated himself and became an important leader in the abolitionist movement. Douglass was a powerful speaker who fought for the civil rights of slaves. He is often called the founder of the American civil rights movement.

civil rights – rights that all citizens have.

abolitionist movement – a movement that wanted to end slavery.

Susan B. Anthony – a strong supporter of women's rights. She is best known as a leader of the women's suffrage movement. Even after she died in 1906, many of her followers kept fighting for suffrage. In 1920, U.S. women finally won the right to vote.

women's suffrage movement – a movement that fought to give women the right to vote.

Mary McLeod Bethune – an educator and civil rights leader. She is best known for starting a school for African American students. The school was successful and became known as Bethune-Cookman College. In 1936, President Franklin Roosevelt made Bethune one of his advisors.

Franklin Roosevelt – president of the United States. He entered office during a very hard time. The nation's economy was hurting. Many U.S. citizens were out of work. Even many people who were once rich lost their homes and became poor. This period was known as the Great Depression. Roosevelt came up with a plan to fix the country's problems. It was called the New Deal. He also led the country through World War II.

New Deal – Roosevelt's plan to fix the country's problems during the Great Depression. The government spent money to make jobs and help the poor. It helped people make it through some of the nation's toughest times.

World War II – The war got its name because it was the second war in twenty-five years to involve many countries. Roosevelt was a strong leader during the war. Under his leadership, the United States and its allies defeated Germany and Japan. Victory in the war helped protect democracy and freedom in the United States and other countries.

Eleanor Roosevelt – the wife of President Franklin Roosevelt. She supported human rights. She became a U.S. delegate to the United Nations. While a member of the U.N., Roosevelt helped write a special declaration on human rights. It was the first international document to ever say that people all over the world have human rights.

human rights - rights that belong to every person and should not be taken away by the government. Eleanor Roosevelt wanted equal rights for minorities and women. She even got her husband to include help for women in some of his New Deal programs.

United Nations – (U.N.) was formed after World War II. Many countries are members. These countries try to prevent wars and meet the needs of people around the world.

Thurgood Marshall – a lawyer who fought for civil rights. In a court case called *Brown v. Board of Education*, Marshall got the Supreme Court to say that segregation in public schools is illegal. Soon, segregation was not allowed in other places either. Marshall became a hero to many. Marshall later became the first African American to sit as a judge on the Supreme Court.

Lyndon B. Johnson – president of the United States from 1963–1969. While he was president, Johnson wanted to end poverty in the United States. He also wanted African Americans and other minorities to be treated fairly. He started a series of programs called the Great Society. These programs tried to help poor people. They provided money, education, and medical help. President Johnson also signed laws that protected civil rights. One of the most important laws he signed was the Voting Rights Act of 1965. This law made it easier for African Americans to register to vote. President Johnson helped open the door for more blacks to vote and serve in elected office.

Cesar Chavez – a Mexican American farm worker. He helped win better rights for migrant workers. Chavez founded the National Farm Workers Association and the United Farm Workers. For many years, Chavez protested poor working conditions and the use of dangerous pesticides. Chavez helped win better pay and treatment for many Hispanic workers.

CHAPTER 2: GEOGRAPHIC UNDERSTANDINGS

Practice 2.1: Major Geographic Features in the United States
Page 34

1. Mississippi   1   Hudson   6
   Missouri   5   Colorado 3
   Rio Grande 4   Ohio   2
2. A

Practice 2.2: Finding Location on Maps and Globes
Page 38

1. A   2. B   3. A   4. C   5. D

Chapter 2 Review
Pages 41–44
Key Terms, People, and Concepts

geography – the study of the earth and its peoples. Geography also includes the mountains, rivers, oceans, and other features that make up the earth's surface.

Mississippi River – the second longest river in the United States. The Mississippi River is one of the most important rivers in U.S. history. It allows travelers and goods to travel back and forth between the Gulf of Mexico to the central United States. Many major cities are located along the Mississippi. The river serves as a dividing line between the eastern and western United States.

Ohio River – runs from Pennsylvania to Illinois. It is a tributary of the Mississippi River. For many years, the Ohio served as a boundary between the British colonies and Native American territory. Later, the Ohio River served as a boundary between slave states and free states. It also played an important role in trade and commerce. People used the Ohio to travel and ship goods from eastern cities to western territories.

Missouri River – a tributary of the Mississippi. It is the longest river in the United States. It runs from Montana to Missouri. The Missouri played an important role as people moved west. It allowed explorers to travel west by water. Later, it allowed travelers and traders to use boats to move from east to west.

Rio Grande – a river that separates Texas from Mexico. It begins in Colorado and runs to the Gulf of Mexico.

Colorado River – a river that runs from the state of Colorado to the Gulf of California in Mexico. Over millions of years, the river's flow has created the Grand Canyon. The Grand Canyon is a deep gorge located in Arizona.

Hudson River – a river that runs through eastern New York. It meets the Atlantic Ocean at New York City. Native Americans and early Europeans used the river for travel and trade. Many early European explorers sailed up the Hudson because they thought it would take them all the way to the Pacific Ocean.

Appalachian Mountains – mountains that run from Georgia to southern Canada. Early British colonists had difficulty crossing the Appalachians. After the American Revolution, many white settlers crossed the Appalachians. Also, many Native Americans lived in and beyond the Appalachian Mountains long before white American settlers arrived.

Rocky Mountains – mountains that are located in the western United States. They run from the state of New Mexico to western Canada. The Rockies were home to Native Americans for thousands of years before white Europeans arrived. Many white settlers moved to the region after people discovered gold during the seventeen and eighteen hundreds.

globes – models of the earth.

maps – flat pictures of the earth, or some part of the earth. People use both to learn where places are located in the world.

latitude – imaginary lines on maps that help people locate places more easily. Lines of latitude run east-west.

longitude - imaginary lines that make it easier to understand where places are. Lines of longitude run north-south from pole to pole.

parallels – lines of latitude are called parallels.

meridians – lines of longitude are called meridians.

equator – the parallel that runs around a globe or across a world map at its center. The equator is located at 0° latitude.

Northern Hemisphere – the northern half of the world. Every parallel above the equator is in the Northern Hemisphere.

Southern Hemisphere – the southern half of the world. Every parallel below the equator is in the Southern Hemisphere.

prime meridian – a meridian that runs from pole to pole through parts of Europe and Africa. It is located at 0 longitude.

International Date Line – the meridian located at 180 longitude. It is located directly opposite of the prime meridian on a globe.

Western Hemisphere – the western half of the world. Every meridian west of the prime meridian up to the International Date Line is located in the Western Hemisphere.

Eastern Hemisphere – the eastern half of the world. Every meridian located east of the prime meridian up to the International Date Line is located in the Eastern Hemisphere.

Multiple Choice Questions
1. B   2. B   3. C   4. A   5. B   6. D   7. B   8. D   9. C

CHAPTER 3: CHARACTER TRAITS OF POSITIVE CITIZENSHIP
Practice 3.1: Principles of Republican Government
Page 50
1. B   2. C   3. A
4. Separation of powers means that power is divided between different branches of government. The founders wanted a separation of power so that no one leader or body of leaders would become too powerful.

Practice 3.2
Page 54 (top)
Responses may vary.

Chapter 3 Review
Pages 54 (bottom)–56
Key Terms, People, and Concepts
U.S. Constitution – the nation's national set of laws. The U.S. Constitution was written in 1787 by the founding fathers. The Constitution tells its readers how the U.S. government works.

separation of powers – The government of the United States is based on separation of powers. Power does not rest with one ruler or group of rulers. Instead, it separates power by dividing it between three branches of government. Separation of powers helps make sure no leader or group of leaders becomes too powerful.

legislative branch – the first branch of government. The legislative branch makes laws.

Congress – the national legislative branch of government. It is made up of two houses.

House of Representatives – one of the houses in the legislative branch of government. It is based on population. States with more people have more representatives. Members of the House of Representatives serve two-year terms. The House has the power to impeach the president and other public officials.

Senate – the second house in Congress. Each state has two senators. Members of the Senate serve six-year terms. The Senate must okay treaties with other countries. It must also okay public officials appointed by the president.

executive branch – the branch of government that enforces the nation's laws. Enforcement means making sure that federal laws are followed.

president – The president of the United States heads the executive branch. He or she is the leader of the country. The president enforces laws, deals with other countries, sets policies, and is commander in chief of the nation's military. The president also appoints federal judges and members of the cabinet.

veto – The president can veto laws passed by Congress. If the president vetoes a law, it does not become a law unless two-thirds of both houses of Congress vote in favor of it again.

vice president – the second highest executive. He or she leads the Senate. But he or she only votes in the Senate if there is a tie to break. If the president dies or is unable to finish his or her term, then the vice president becomes president. Both the president and the vice president serve four-year terms.

cabinet – the executive branch also includes the president's cabinet. The cabinet is not mentioned in the Constitution. Cabinet members give the president advice and are in charge of different parts of the executive branch.

judicial branch – is made up of courts. The courts make sure that laws follow the Constitution and are applied fairly.

United States Supreme Court – the highest court in the United States. The president appoints members of the Supreme Court and all lower federal courts. Nine justices sit on the Supreme Court.

chief justice – the lead justice on the U.S. Supreme Court.

appeals – An appeal is a court case that has already been decided by a lower court. It is reviewed by the Supreme Court to make sure that the case was decided correctly and that all laws were followed. Most cases that the U.S. Supreme Court hears are appeals.

federal government – is the national government (Congress, the president, and the federal courts).

state governments – responsible for state matters. They have a certain amount of power to decide on state laws.

General Assembly – In Georgia, the legislative branch is called the General Assembly. The General Assembly makes the state's laws.

governor – serves as Georgia's chief executive. The governor is responsible for enforcing state laws. Like the president, he or she may choose to veto laws. He or she also acts as the commander in chief of Georgia's National Guard.

Georgia Supreme Court – the state's highest court. State courts make sure Georgia's state and local laws are fair and follow the state constitution.

local governments – responsible for counties, cities, and towns.

county commissions – a county government. It serves as a local legislative branch of government.

city/town councils – city/town governments that serve as legislative branches. Citizens usually elect the people who serve on these bodies. Local legislative bodies pass local laws and deal with local policies.

mayors, county managers, and **city managers** – act as local executives. Sometimes citizens directly elect these executives. Sometimes the local legislative branch appoints them.

cooperation – a positive character trait of good citizens and leaders. When people cooperate, they work together to solve problems. For example, Frederick Douglass cooperated with white abolitionists to tell people about the evils of slavery. During the Great Depression, President Roosevelt cooperated with Congress and other leaders to deal with economic challenges. During the 1960s, President Lyndon Johnson cooperated with Congress and civil rights leaders to pass civil rights laws and laws meant to end poverty. Poor, immigrant farm workers cooperated and worked together under the leadership of Cesar Chavez to win better conditions for laborers.

diligence – People who are diligent work hard and with great focus. They pursue goals wisely. Women like Susan B. Anthony showed great diligence in the way they organized the women's suffrage movement. They stayed focused and worked hard in the face of great challenges. Their diligence led to women winning the right to vote nationally in 1920.

liberty – the freedom to act and believe the way you want to. Many historical figures became heroes because they defended liberty. For example, Thurgood Marshall became a hero of the civil rights movement. As a lawyer, he stood up and fought for the liberty of an African American girl to attend an all-white school. Later, as the first African American on the Supreme Court, he continued to stand up for liberty by protecting peoples' rights under the Constitution.

justice – People who value justice seek equal treatment under the law for everyone. Eleanor Roosevelt stood up for human rights. Frederick Douglass fought to end slavery. Thurgood Marshall stood up to racism. Lyndon Johnson sought to protect the rights of the poor and minorities. Cesar Chavez fought for justice for migrant workers.

tolerance – Tolerant people respect people's right to believe differently than they do. The United States is full of many different kinds of people. Tolerance is important for making sure people get along.

freedom of conscience and expression – Freedom of conscience means the freedom to think and feel the way you want. Freedom of expression is the freedom to express how you think and feel. People express things in different ways. Some say how they feel through speeches or protests. Some write how they feel or what they believe in newspapers or books. Colonists who favored independence at the time of the American Revolution, women who marched for suffrage, and many other U.S. citizens have exercised freedom of conscience and expression.

respect for authority – Authority means being in charge. The federal government has authority over the nation. State governments have authority over states. Teachers have authority over students. And parents have authority over children. People who respect authority accept the authority over them. Sometimes, historical figures have not accepted authority. Paul Revere and other supporters of the American Revolution did not accept England's authority over the colonies. Frederick Douglass did not accept slaveholders' authority over African American slaves. Cesar Chavez did not accept the authority of farmers over Hispanic migrant workers.

Multiple Choice Questions
1. D   2. B   3. D   4. D   5. A   6. D   7. C   8. C

5

CHAPTER 4: ECONOMIC UNDERSTANDINGS
Practice 4.1: Producing Goods and Services
Page 62
1. B   2. A   3. C   4. D   5. A

Practice 4.2: Economic Interdependence and Personal Money Choices
Page 65
1. C
2. It is easier and cheaper than making everything themselves.
3. *Responses may vary.*

Chapter 4 Review
Pages 66–68
Key Terms and Concepts
economy - what businesses sell, what people buy, and how businesses, governments, and people spend their money all affect the economy.
producers – make things. People, businesses, and government can all be producers.
consumers – buy the things producers make. People, businesses, and government can all be consumers.
goods – some producers make goods. Goods are things you can hold. Hats, bikes, cheeseburgers, and cell phones are all goods.
services – some producers provide services. Services are things you pay for but can't hold. When a doctor examines you, he or she is providing a service. When sanitation workers pick up your trash, they are providing a service.
resources – things that a person, government, or business has. Resources can be used to produce things. They can also be used to buy things. Money is a resource.
land – an important resource. Land includes the natural ground that a person or building stands on. It also includes the buildings themselves.
labor – the work that people do. Bagging groceries is a form of labor. Fixing cars and typing on a computer are labor as well. Teaching students, answering phones, and the jobs your parents do are all labor. It takes labor to produce things.
capital goods – goods that are used to produce other things. Machines in a factory are examples of capital. Trucks that haul things to stores, the computer used to write this book, and staplers used in an office are all capital goods.
entrepreneur – someone who starts a business. Entrepreneurs raise the money to start a business and decide what the business will produce. Entrepreneurs take great risk. If their business does well, they can make lots of money. If their business does not do well, they could lose money. Entrepreneurs are very important in the U.S. economy. Without entrepreneurs, there would be no businesses.
market economy – In a market economy, there are producers and consumers. Consumers will only pay up to a certain price for a good or service. In a market economy, producers sell goods and services at the highest price consumers will pay. If the highest price consumers will pay does not give the producer a profit, then producers will stop producing the good or service. The government provides some goods and services. These services are very important, but might not be provided by businesses. The national government provides a military to protect the country. It also provides interstate highways. State governments provide state roads and schools. Local governments provide libraries, police departments, and fire departments. Governments also provide parks and other special services.
price – the amount of money consumers pay for goods or services. Producers want to produce things that have a high price. Consumers want to buy things that have a low price.
profit – the amount of money producers make after paying to produce their good or service.
fees – money that people pay the government to use a good or service.
fines – money people pay the government as punishment for breaking a law. Paying $50 for a speeding ticket is an example of a fine.
taxes – money people and businesses have to pay the government. People have to pay taxes on their income, their homes, and many other things. Businesses have to pay taxes on the profits they make. The number-one way the government pays for things is through taxes.
interdependence – to depend on each other. In the U.S. economy, consumers and producers are interdependent. Consumers depend on producers to make things. Producers depend on consumers to buy the things. Without producers, consumers would have to make everything they need themselves. Without consumers, producers could not make money.

trade – when different parts of the country or world sell goods to each other. Different areas trade with each other because it is easier than trying to make everything themselves. People in different places are better at producing different things. Countries can often buy goods from other nations for less money than producing it at home. Trade makes different parts of the country and world economically interdependent.

currency – anything that is accepted as money. Dollars are currency in the United States. Before countries can trade with one another, they have to know how much the currency in one country is worth in another country.

spending – When people buy things, they are spending money. The good part about spending money is that people get the things they want or need right away. The bad part about spending money is that, after people spend it, the money is gone.

saving – When people keep their money to use later, they are saving money. The bad part about saving money is that people have to do without things they would like to buy. The good part about saving money is that they have the money to buy other things later. People often save money to buy things that they cannot afford to buy right away. People save money to buy houses, retire from work, or to take a nice trip.

Multiple Choice Questions
1. A   2. B   3. C   4. B   5. B   6. C   7. C   8. B

PRACTICE TEST 1
Pages 69–86

1. D	11. C	21. C	31. C	41. B	51. A	61. C
2. D	12. C	22. A	32. A	42. B	52. A	62. D
3. A	13. A	23. B	33. B	43. A	53. A	63. C
4. B	14. B	24. D	34. C	44. D	54. C	64. C
5. C	15. A	25. B	35. B	45. A	55. C	65. A
6. B	16. B	26. B	36. B	46. A	56. B	66. B
7. B	17. C	27. C	37. D	47. B	57. C	67. B
8. C	18. A	28. A	38. A	48. D	58. D	68. A
9. D	19. A	29. B	39. A	49. B	59. B	69. C
10. B	20. B	30. A	40. C	50. B	60. A	70. B

PRACTICE TEST 2
Pages 87–103

1. B	11. C	21. A	31. C	41. C	51. A	61. C
2. A	12. C	22. B	32. B	42. B	52. C	62. A
3. A	13. A	23. A	33. B	43. C	53. A	63. C
4. C	14. C	24. B	34. A	44. B	54. B	64. C
5. B	15. A	25. B	35. C	45. A	55. D	65. C
6. C	16. A	26. A	36. D	46. C	56. D	66. B
7. B	17. A	27. B	37. C	47. B	57. C	67. A
8. A	18. C	28. C	38. B	48. A	58. D	68. A
9. A	19. D	29. C	39. B	49. B	59. B	69. B
10. B	20. B	30. B	40. D	50. C	60. A	70. D